NOBODY CARES ABOUT YOUR UNIVERSITY... YET.

Second Edition
Featuring New Winning
Strategies for Marketers

DR. SEAN CARTON AND ANDRES ZAPATA

ISBN 978-0-578-59523-8

Proudly published and printed in
Baltimore, Maryland, USA.
idfive.com

TABLE OF CONTENTS

Introduction | 1

The OpenEDU Marketing Model | 11

Internal Assessment | 21

The Forces: Understanding Your Initial Conditions | 35

Research | 55

Defining Your Audiences | 67

The Creative Process | 89

The First Pillar: Traffic | 103

The Second Pillar: Destination | 131

The Third Pillar: Nurture | 151

Looking Forward: Where Data-Driven Marketing Is Leading | 159

Conclusion | 171

Appendix 1: Being a Good Client | 177

Appendix 2: Research Resources | 185

ACKNOWLEDGMENTS

A book like this doesn't happen overnight and it doesn't get done without a lot of help. We would like to acknowledge the expert contributions from Anthony D. Paul, Taylor Jade Powell, Paige Wheeler, and Alan Carl.

Finally, we would like to thank our clients. This book wouldn't have been possible without your support, collaboration, and belief in the OpenEDU Model over the years.

FOREWORD

"What does the 'id' in 'idfive' stand for?"

This is the most common question we get asked whenever we're meeting with new potential clients.

"Informed design," we answer. "It's at the core of what we do."

When we formed idfive in January of 2008, we did so with one guiding principle: We wanted everything we did for our clients to be based on insights driven by research. We didn't want to be like all the other digital agencies we saw out there, flying by the seats of their collective pants, going with their "guts" and hoping for the best. Instead, we wanted to create an agency where data informed the marketing plans and research informed the design, so that we could point to every element on the page and every pixel on the screen and tell our clients exactly why it was there.

That's the kind of agency we created. But our commitment to basing creative decisions on a deep understanding of our clients, their goals, their audiences, and those audiences' motivations didn't start when we founded idfive. The roots of our philosophy go back another decade, to the crazy days of the late 90's dot-com boom and to a large East Coast research university looking to build a "real" website for the first time.

Today, when digital is the norm and even the tiniest institution wouldn't dream of not having an online presence, it's hard to imagine a time when many colleges and universities considered it a gamble to commit resources to a comprehensive institutional website. But that's how it was, and, just as strangely, many marketing and communications departments had to fight to have any say in their institution's website. "It's a computer thing, right?" we heard from so many. "The IT department's going to take care of it."

That was the situation that Andres and I found ourselves facing at our former agency where I headed up the interactive practice. Somehow, against all odds (or so it seemed), we'd been hired to build the first "real" website for one of the best-known universities in the world. We knew it was going to be a huge job and, having already worked with a few other institutions of higher learning, we also knew it was going to be an exercise in diplomacy, requiring us to build consensus in an institution with a (well-deserved) reputation for independent thought and a decentralized structure.

Nothing embodied this ethos more than the website the institution had when they hired our firm. Since first going online, the site had expanded like a coral reef, bursting forth from those on campus — IT geeks, academics, graduate students, and forward-thinking staff — who saw the potential in this whole new "web thing."

At the time, the concept of web governance was basically non-existent and most institutions saw their websites as internal communication vehicles with limited utility when it came to communicating with peer institutions and research partners. Our client was no different and employed a, shall we say, *laissez-faire* attitude when it came to adding new links to the homepage. If a campus unit wanted a link on the homepage, they could add it as long as they didn't mind it being at the bottom of a rapidly growing and long-scrolling homepage. How long? When we printed it out, it was eight feet long.

But as weird as this sounds today — and, frankly, as weird as it sounded back then — the "system" that led to the eight-foot homepage fit the free-wheeling, decentralized philosophy of the university. As a result, there was a lot of resistance on campus to changing anything about it. If it ain't broke, don't fix it, right? Andres and I still have flashbacks about some of those early web committee meetings we had to brave.

But we pushed onwards. We knew the institution wasn't taking the right approach to creating a website of the size and stature of this one. But how to convince the web committee?

The answer came from an unexpected place: the website's analytics. When we ran the rudimentary analytics package that was available at the time, we noticed something fascinating. While links that appeared on the first couple of screens of the homepage drove a lot of traffic to their destinations, the links farther down received no clicks at all. The late arrivals at the bottom of the eight-foot page may have gotten much-coveted homepage exposure but it wasn't doing them a lick of good. Nobody scrolled down that far. Nobody even knew they were there.

Bingo. We had our answer. Using metrics, we had found the insight — and the data to back it up — we needed to win our case for creating a more organized homepage featuring a few main categories that led to sets of links like in the websites we're familiar with today.

We convinced the web committee and got the go-ahead to build the website that the institution needed. Informed design won. And it's still winning today.

The principles we formed way back when and have honed over the years have gone into developing our OpenEDU Marketing Model — the model that's at the core of this book. Obviously, the world of higher ed marketing is a lot different today than it was at the turn of the millennium. But even though we're sure that most anyone reading this is more sophisticated about marketing than was our client of 20 years ago, there has never been a time when it's been more important for everyone involved in higher ed to enhance their understanding of how to recruit and retain students. Times are tough. And they're going to get tougher.

That's why we wrote this book the first time and why we thought it was so important to put out this second edition in the early months of 2020. The response we received when we shared our OpenEDU Model the first time was phenomenal, but 2020 is looking a lot different than 2016.[1] Not only are new technologies like artificial intelligence and Big Data transforming the way marketing is done, but we're now looking at a whole new generation of prospective students. And Gen Z is shaping up to be quite a different cohort than the millennials.

But Gen Z is just part of the consideration. The entire face of higher education is changing as institutions seek new markets to replace the shrinking pool of international students and the smaller pool of traditional undergraduates. "Non-traditional" is becoming the "new-traditional." Competition for online students is becoming even fiercer as some of the for-profit institutions that dominated just a few years ago are losing ground to the wave of non-profit and state institutions coming online, often driven behind the scenes by for-profit OPMs (Online Program Managers) who can take even the stodgiest institution online in just a few months. Add to all of this the growing concerns about ballooning student debt, political polarization, and an expanding industry of alternatives to the traditional four-year degree (and new formats for graduate degrees that promise to provide credentials faster, easier, and cheaper than ever before) and it's clear that, as higher ed marketers, our jobs have never been tougher.

Even if you've read the first edition of *Nobody Cares About Your University...Yet*, we hope that you'll take the time to read this second edition. It's been reorganized, expanded, and is now even more laser-focused on providing you with the tools you need to succeed in tough times. We've trimmed back on some of the big picture stuff so that we could provide even more practical, actionable advice and included a whole new suite of tools that you can use today to improve your practice and make your marketing even more effective and efficient. We've even included some new chapters to bring you up to speed on the latest marketing technologies so that you'll be prepared for what's to come.

Let's do it!

There has never been a time
when it's been more important for
everyone involved in higher ed to
enhance their understanding of
how to recruit and retain students.

INTRODUCTION

Conventional wisdom says that everyone who can go to college should go to college. However, that falls apart when someone asks why. Is it to train for a job? Learn critical thinking and communication skills? Make lifelong friends? Network with alumni? Join a fraternity or sorority? Find a particular academic field of study worthy of dogged pursuit? Get out of your parents' house?

Traditional colleges and universities offer all of the above. They're all-inclusive destinations ostensibly focused on the transmission of information from those who know to those who don't. But somehow, in the practice of that mission, many graduates face crippling debt and limited job prospects after commencement. Other students drift through campus for a semester or two, find little in the way of inspiration, and move on. Some even manage to mire themselves in debt without getting a degree.

Higher education underserves a lot of students. And even though the industry — and, yes, it's an industry — grew exponentially over the 20th- and early 21st-centuries, many people are currently questioning whether higher education is really delivering on its promises. Or if maybe it's no longer worth the cost.

Other industries face similar challenges. Witness the boom and bust cycles of the American automotive, broadcast, and retail sectors. They too have struggled to stay relevant in an era marked by dramatic technological, cultural, demographic, and economic changes.

Amid the current state of upheaval, are today's colleges destined to become yet another endangered bastion of brick-and-mortar-based American ingenuity? Maybe. But even within a global "new normal" of constant turmoil, we firmly believe that there are opportunities for our institutions to evolve and thrive.

Our take on higher education — how we got here and, more importantly, how to adapt — is grounded in more than two decades of experience working with colleges and universities. We've collaborated with faculty and staff, navigated internal politics, and applied proven strategies to increase our clients' return on investment. We understand your challenges. And we believe in your potential.

Our playbook, the OpenEDU Marketing Model, is based on proven industry principles and the philosophy of open-source software. Knowledge like this should be free. Take it, share it, and modify it as needed.[2]

We hope you'll use these ideas to connect with your audiences more effectively and to inspire new groups to reconsider the value of higher education. It's a commitment borne by care and concern.

However, before we dive into the OpenEDU Model and its application, we want to clear up a few terms that we'll be using a lot throughout this book.

Strategy vs. Tactics

The difference between "strategy" and "tactics" is a persistent classroom stumper. It can be understood in as many ways as there are people thinking about it. Many of the definitions stop just short of being flat-out wrong and land in the nebulous territory of "functionally adequate." Perhaps as a result of this, "strategy" versus "tactics" is misunderstood often enough to warrant clarification.

Here's an easy way to understand the difference:

"Strategy" is where you want to go.

"Tactics" are the roads you can take to get there.

In terms that apply to the OpenEDU Model, "strategy" is the "big idea" behind a campaign, why you want to say what you want to say (and to whom). "Tactics" are the different ways to do that.

As an example, let's say you have a waffle shop and want to increase revenue. Your *strategy* might be to attract additional business (why) by emphasizing the versatility of your waffles as a food one could eat at any meal (what) to potential new customers (whom). How you get that message out — an email marketing campaign to a list of people in your area who have purchased frozen waffles in the past, a drive-time radio campaign encouraging people to stop by and pick up waffles for dinner, or a giant waffle-shaped balloon floating over your shop touting "Waffles! Hot and ready NOW, good for breakfast, lunch, dinner, or a late-night snack" — are all *tactics* that could serve the strategy you created.

But you're not a waffle shop. If you were, we could probably stop here. Instead, we want to address another term that can give people trouble.

Branding

Many people treat the concept of brand as if it's ineffable. However, treating a foundational idea as if it's too grand to describe is not helpful. So, let us offer this definition:

Brand *is*.

Yup. It's as simple as that. Your institution's brand exists whether or not anyone's taken active steps to create it. If you have an institution, you have a brand.

The concept may sound strange to anyone who still perceives "brand" — as derived from the marks that ranchers seared into their cattle — as being a well-defined visual representation. Does that describe your viewpoint? It might. If you still use "brand" as a stand-in for your logo or if you talk about branding as a design exercise, you're still clinging to the idea that brand and logo are closely related, if not synonymous. And if you think that, you probably also think that controlling your institution's brand begins and ends by adhering strictly to a set of guidelines and keeping a close watch on how various academic and administrative units use (some say "butcher," but we think that's harsh) your institution's logo, color palette, or, in some cases, tagline.

The reality is, your brand is a lot more complex than what gets expressed in your brand guidelines. In fact, many people misunderstand the concept of brand because they flip the relationship between the visual representations of the brand (logos, colors, etc.) and the actual experience of the brand itself. The design elements of your brand don't *create* your brand — as we said before, your brand exists whether anyone has taken the time to create it or not — but those elements can be linked to the brand experience so that they come to represent the brand to those who encounter them in the marketplace.

Think of brands working like words. Whether we call a fuzzy, four-legged pet a dog or *le chien* or *el perro*, it remains the same animal. The sound and spelling of a word, by itself, is meaningless. It's the relationship we create between a word and an object that matters. Somewhere in the distant past of English-speaking people, the word dog got linked to the animal so that evoking the word now evokes the feeling of the animal. Our jobs as marketers is to create the same kinds of connections when it comes to branding. In order for a logo (or anything else in a brand guide) to evoke a feeling in consumers, you first have to attach a unique meaning to your brand.

To learn how that works, let's take a brief detour and look at where the whole concept of brand got wrapped up in the practice of marketing.

Linguistics and Listerine

The story of Joseph Lawrence's invention is a great place to start when explaining how brands and branding work. Lawrence was a 19th-century American who was smitten by two recent scientific breakthroughs: Louis Pasteur's ideas about infection and Joseph Lister's discovery that carbolic acid could be used to kill germs. Lawrence developed a mixture that seemed to do as good a job of killing germs as carbolic acid. He licensed the formula to a pharmacist, Jordan Wheat Lambert, in 1881. In honor of Lister's work, the Lambert Pharmacal Company began marketing the mixture as Listerine. They promoted it as a wonder formula for everything from cleaning your floors to cleaning your, ahem, nether regions to making your breath sparkling fresh.

Unfortunately for Lambert, Americans didn't think they had a problem with bad breath. It just wasn't a thing ... until Jordan Lambert's son, Gerard, came along.

Gerard Lambert realized that, if Americans didn't think they had bad breath, he needed to convince them that they did. While digging into medical literature, he chanced upon the term "halitosis," a previously obscure word used mainly by doctors who needed to describe particularly bad breath. Gerard then launched a barrage of advertising designed to "educate" the public about a problem they didn't even know they had: chronic halitosis.

Gerard Lambert's campaign relentlessly called out the social problems associated with bad breath. Mothers were told that their children secretly couldn't stand to be around them because their breath stank. Young men and women were told that nobody wanted to marry them because their mouths smelled like sewers. Women with bad breath were painted as social outcasts whose friends talked about them behind their backs. Who would want to be near someone whose breath made them sick?

The impact of the campaign was immediate and spectacular. In seven years, sales of Listerine shot up from $118,000 to more than $8 million.[3] Halitosis — a condition nobody knew they had before the campaign — became a household word. Modern advertising was born! And Listerine was on its way.

Nowadays, the Listerine campaign seems unsophisticated and rather offensive. But it does provide an excellent lesson on branding. By taking a word that was unknown to the general public (and therefore neutral when it came to any emotional associations) and linking it to shame, social ostracism, bad health, and general failure, Lambert was able to construct a reality in which halitosis became Public Enemy #1, and Listerine was the only product to cure it.

Note that presenting Listerine as a generic cleaning product wasn't nearly as successful as was presenting it as a scientifically derived cure for bad breath (and a cure for the social stigma that came with it). Why? Because branding can't make you all things to all people. Nor can it make you something you're not. A dog would be the same animal no matter its name. But once someone *gave* it a name, that name and the animal became inextricably linked.

If you identify what makes your organization or product unique (or what you can reasonably claim makes you unique) you can "own" that by linking a name and brand elements like a logo and color pallete to the unique aspect of your brand. The logo and everything else in your brand guide don't create your brand; they are the symbols that evoke the feeling of your brand *after* you've done the work of identifying and creating your brand. If you don't do that work, then your brand symbols won't represent anything. And instead of having control over the creation of your brand, you'll leave that creation up to the whims of the marketplace, with consumers attaching their own meaning to your brand.

When Listerine launched, there was no other product that fought bad breath, and certainly no other scientifically derived product. As such, they were able to make Listerine *mean* "the scientific cure for bad breath." That became their (highly successful) brand.

Of course, you're not a mouthwash manufacturer any more than you are a waffle shop. So, let's talk about you and take a look at the OpenEDU Model.

—

Your institution's brand exists whether or not anyone's taken active steps to create it. If you have an institution, you have a brand.

THE OPENEDU
MARKETING MODEL

Most college or university marketing strategies start life facing a dizzying array of challenges: shifting market forces, paralyzing internal politics, unrealistic timelines, and inadequate funding. Developing a marketing strategy can be risky, and that risk compounds at each stage of follow-through. But no matter how much risk you face, the risks associated with inaction are almost always greater. So, you have to move forward.

The good news? The task is not impossible. You just need to manage the risks you face. That's why we developed the OpenEDU Model.

The model is based on years of hard work and more than a few hard knocks. We have spent decades testing and tweaking various strategic models and studying just about everything out there on strategy, branding, and marketing. We even interviewed experts at other marketing firms, ensuring that the OpenEDU Model is indeed "open."

The result is a synthesis of proven principles and innovative ideas from many brilliant and talented marketers who preceded us. We're standing on the shoulders of giants, and now we want to share the view. We believe that models like this should be free and available because we're all trying to accomplish the same thing: education.

The OpenEDU Model is designed to be as simple as possible to understand and implement. While there's a fair amount of complexity in its various modules, the main ideas at the core of the model are designed to be clear, communicable, and succinct.

In this section, we'll introduce the central concepts of the OpenEDU Model. The rest of the book will give you the details you need to put it to work.

The Anatomy of the OpenEDU Model

Think of the OpenEDU Model as a simplified representation of a building. The structure has a foundation upon which rest three pillars that support a single roof. Simple, right?

The foundation of this structure is your *brand platform*. As we mentioned earlier, your institution has a brand, whether you've devoted energy to creating it or not. But when we talk about brand platform, we're specifically talking about the brand image you've chosen for yourself.

In the same way that Listerine branded itself as a scientifically derived cure for the stigma of bad breath, you need a fundamental "truth" to convey to the world. Most likely, you already know what this truth is and have been building it/maintaining it for years. But it's worth taking some time to reexamine your brand platform and ensure it's strong enough to hold up an entire marketing campaign.

How do you know if your brand platform is strong enough? Like any good foundation, it should be built for the terrain you're on. The brand platform of a small private liberal arts college needs to be different than the brand platform of a large public university. A school with an emphasis on STEM fields needs a brand platform different than one focused on the arts. And it gets a lot more specific when you factor in your institution's location, religious affiliation (if there is one), admissions requirements, campus design, date of founding, tuition costs, athletic opportunities, and every other way your school differs from other schools.

However, you shouldn't stop with a list of differences, no matter how long it is. Consider what those differences *mean* for your audience. The better you understand why and how your differences can attract students, faculty, donors, and others, the better you can transform those differences into a coherent and reality-based brand.

We're not saying that you shouldn't be aspirational about who you are or that you shouldn't present your brand in a positive manner. You can — and should — do those things. As long as you understand that you can't successfully present yourself as something that you're not and aren't planning to become. That's like trying to build a skyscraper on a marsh. Eventually, things will collapse.

Fortunately, if your school is doing a good job of being a school, a lot of the branding work has been done for you. You can find the brand in the look of the campus, in the way the admissions office answers the phone, and in the yearly traditions. And, most notably, you can find the brand in the special way that alumni, faculty, and students feel whenever they encounter your institution, no matter where they are. Your goal as a marketer is to communicate that feeling to those who aren't familiar with it. Because that feeling — grounded in a unique reality — is your brand platform. And, upon it, you can support the next level of the OpenEDU Model: the three pillars of traffic, destination, and nurture.

Those three pillars are the most important areas of tactical focus in your marketing campaign. Later in the book, we'll discuss each in depth, but here's a quick overview.

- **TRAFFIC:** This is the attention you generate from your marketing activities. Typically made up of advertising, signage, social media, etc., the traffic pillar is about creating general brand awareness and encouraging your audience to take a specific action like visiting a website or registering for an open house. Generating traffic often takes up the bulk of a marketing budget.

- **DESTINATION:** This is the endpoint for your traffic. The destination can be anything from a landing page on the web to a counselor answering the phone in your admissions office. When you generate attention and drive traffic, you want that traffic to go somewhere.

- **NURTURE:** This is the action that occurs once your traffic reaches a destination. Nurturing requires a long-term concerted effort to usher those arrivals toward desired outcomes. Examples include a series of emails designed to move a prospect from interest to enrollment, a set of mailings intended to help parents understand why they should encourage their student to enroll at your institution, or a batch of reminders sent to prospects who expressed an interest in attending your open house. Nurturing is any action that enhances your relationship with your audience.

These three pillars hold up the roof of our structure: the integrated marketing strategy, which encompasses all the activities (tactics) that you employ to achieve your desired outcome.

Of course, no building exists in a vacuum. Wind, water, gravity, and the people who use the building are factors an actual building needs to

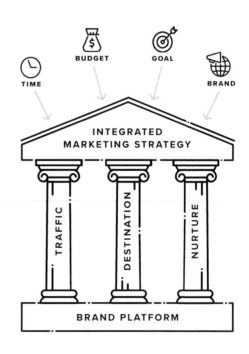

address. Additionally, the building's development might be enhanced or constrained by a variety of site-specific situational factors, such as zoning laws, sustainability goals, or neighborhood aesthetic guidelines.

Our OpenEDU building also needs to accommodate external factors and situations. We call these external factors "forces." As we will do with every element in our model, we'll devote more time to the forces later in the book. But, in brief, the four forces bearing down on the OpenEDU Model are:

- **BUDGET**: How much money is allocated to set and execute the strategy?
- **TIME**: When is the deadline to implement the strategy?
- **GOAL**: What specifically are you trying to accomplish in the short-term and long-term?
- **BRAND PERCEPTION**: How do people feel when they come into contact with your institution?

In the OpenEDU Model, the three pillars (traffic, destination, nurture) are grounded by the foundation (brand platform) and in support of a single, unified roof (integrated marketing strategy). Together, they can withstand the forces around them. We didn't decide on this conceptualization because we wanted a cute, emoji-ready Greek-temple-looking thing to represent our model. It's deliberate.

We want you to remember two key points:

1. Everything you do must be grounded on your brand platform.
2. You must have a strong, well-constructed integrated marketing strategy that overlies the tactics you use to implement it.

And we want to emphasize the importance of this with a structure designed so that it would fall apart if you removed any of its elements. We promised a pretty simple model. But the devil's in the details.

Case Study:
The OpenEDU
Model in Action

The best way to understand how the OpenEDU Model works is to see it in action.

A business school at a major East Coast university hired us after its fifth academic year. Like almost every school, they needed to boost their enrollment. But the need was particularly acute because the school was young and relatively unproven. Even though they had a major university brand behind them, this was a new frontier: the high-stakes, highly competitive world of graduate business education. They needed to gain a foothold. And they needed to grab on fast.

We began our engagement by working to understand their situation — and the general condition of graduate business education — as thoroughly as possible. We conducted discussion groups with faculty, students, staff, and prospects and triangulated the feedback with third-party environmental research to develop a clear picture of the school's brand and value proposition. We also worked hard to develop a better understanding of audience segmentation. This was no small task considering they offered programs appealing to local, regional, and international audiences.

This research led us to the development of the first piece of the OpenEDU puzzle: the brand platform. We recognized the global nature of the school along with the shared values of the institution, which put people first. It was a strong differentiator — business schools aren't exactly known for caring. And it rang true due to the university's record of distinction in the health professions and sciences.

Once we had a solid foundation to work with, we developed a strategy that emphasized structured flexibility and focused primarily on digital media. Digital is so responsive and flexible that we were able to use the data we gathered from our marketing efforts to measure and fine-tune our approach as close to real-time as possible.

The three pillars supported this strategy. Targeted, online display advertising and paid search drove traffic to a destination of program-specific landing pages. An interactive program finder helped guide prospective students to the programs that best fit their needs. It also helped us capture additional data about prospect interests.

After a prospect contacted the school, we nurtured the new relationship with a series of personalized emails and mailings. Whether a prospect requested information or wanted to attend an open house, we worked closely with admissions to develop a program that helped keep that person engaged during the long decision-making period typical of graduate school. We gradually moved them to apply and enroll.

Of course, we operated under a number of constraints, not the least of which was our promise to be held accountable for stewardship of the budget. This required regular feedback about results and close collaboration with our in-house partners in making decisions about how to fine-tune the program for the greatest response. We were also under time-oriented pressure since the client needed to drive enrollments up as soon as possible.

Our joint goal was to focus on response and conversion first and worry about building brand awareness over time as the program progressed. Finally, while we had the brand equity of a world-class university working in our favor, we knew that execution needed to be flawless in order to deliver a brand experience that matched the expectations of the target audiences.

The result? During the first five years, leads increased 903% and enrollments went up 83.14%. Meanwhile, the budget remained relatively flat. We had captured so much data during the program that we were also able to go back and analyze the direct impact our marketing efforts had on enrollments. The results were clear: The plan worked.

And that wasn't even the best news. Prior to working with us, the business school's cost-per-lead was in the hundreds of dollars. Our most recent work has gotten that cost-per-lead down to $28 per highly qualified prospect.

By starting with brand platform, developing a data-driven marketing strategy, and applying strong tactics to hold it up — all while remaining mindful of the constraints of time, budget, goals, and brand — we helped this business school take flight. That's the power of the OpenEDU Model.

INTERNAL ASSESSMENT

21

As discussed, the OpenEDU Model approaches building a marketing plan similar to constructing a physical building. But building a quality structure requires more than just choosing a plan and selecting materials. Before any of that begins, you must select a suitable location and prepare the ground to ensure the stability of the eventual construction. Marketing plans aren't any different: They must incorporate a thorough survey of the "lay of the land" to succeed.

This means conducting a review of all of the aspects of your future campaign that you may not be able to control. We mentioned the four forces earlier — and

Starting with the right information — and obtaining consensus about that information — is a smart way to proceed. To help you gather the information you need, we've created a handy Internal Assessment Questions Worksheet that you can use to make sure you have the info you need to start your planning off right. You can find the worksheet at: nobodycares.idfive.com.

we'll be taking a closer look at those later — but, for now, we're looking at the ground we're building on. Ground as in dirt. As in the nitty-gritty.

Before constructing your foundational brand platform, overarching strategy, and supportive tactical pillars, you must conduct two areas of research to "prepare the ground" — internal and external. We address this first because we have found that it's best to understand as much as possible about what you're working with before proceeding.

Internal Assessment: Yes, You Have To

The most challenging part of developing and executing a successful strategy is looking at yourself and asking the hard questions. Nobody likes to do this in their lives outside of work, and they certainly don't like doing it when surrounded by their colleagues.

Why? Because asking questions like, "Why are we doing this?" requires thinking hard about things that tend to make people uncomfortable. Difficult questions force you and your team to look closely at your institutional culture. Are you doing what you're doing because that's the way it's always been done? Are you doing it because it was dictum from on high, possibly ordered by someone who may not have the best marketing instincts or has incorrect information? Are you doing what you're doing because nobody's spoken up and offered a better idea?

While self-examination is painful, there is a trick that can make it easier: Focus on offering *negative* options. If you want to test this out, use the negative approach the next time you're standing around with your colleagues, trying to decide where to go for lunch. Typically, choosing where to go can be a nightmare because nobody wants to step on anyone else's toes (or expose themselves to criticism) by suggesting a destination. Eventually, one person, driven mad by hunger and frustration, declares a choice. Everyone follows suit, glad to be done with the polite (and highly irritating) group indecision.

However, if you ask for suggestions on where *not* to go, you'll face a very different dynamic. In this scenario, everyone will eagerly make their preferences known by listing the places where they don't want to go. Once everyone has had their say, there are generally no objections to the limited number of choices that are left. Bingo! Decision made!

Eliminating what's not going to work often leads you to what will work. As Sherlock Holmes said in *The Sign of the Four*, "How often have I said to you that when you have eliminated the impossible, whatever remains, however improbable, must be the truth?"

Elementary, dear reader. Keep this approach in mind as you undergo the following internal assessment.

The Nine Key Questions

While admissions, marketing, and student services are often divided into silos on campus — working with different priorities, leadership, and budgets — together, they are responsible for the total tuition revenue. That means, for a marketing plan to succeed, all of the parties will need to share some semblance of a unified vision and approach. However, before you can get to where you want to go, you have to know where you are.

Start by inviting every stakeholder to answer the following questions. These prompts are designed to build consensus about what problems exist and why they exist, which can give you a preliminary glimpse into the brand platform, strategy, and tactics that are best suited to the reality of your institution.

You may make people uncomfortable during the process. That's great. When you're probing assumptions and evaluating existing systems, you can't take anything for granted. Just remember that you're challenging constraints, not the people bound to them.

If you and your colleagues are honest and thorough in this phase, you will eventually be able to create a shared vision and a sound, defensible plan for making it happen. So be brave; it's worth it.

1. What happens if we do nothing?

This question should be the first one asked at any meeting, or at least before starting any new initiative. It forces you to confront reality based on current conditions and trends. If enrollments are down and the pool of prospective students is shrinking, it won't be hard to see what maintaining the status quo will lead to.

2. What are we trying to accomplish?

Whenever we tackle a problem, we see it through the lens of our own experience. Marketers may think of recruitment as brand awareness. Admissions might prioritize contact with prospects. Student affairs departments might focus on campus life. And faculty members may pay attention to the pedagogical experience. It's in our nature to do this, but we should strive to look outside of our own disciplines when tackling a problem. How? Stick to specific, measurable answers. Record benchmarks, quantify goals, and set deadlines. If it can't be measured, don't do it.

3. What does success look like?

By defining success as explicitly as possible, you can set initial benchmarks and ongoing milestones. Plus, you can explain why the measures you're using are important. Let's say your answer to Question #2 is, "Increase enrollment by 20% over five years." Great. Now define precisely how you want that to happen. What is the current enrollment? How and when will an increase occur? Is it acceptable if enrollments are flat for four years but you hit your goal in year five? Is it realistic to expect an annual increase of 4%? Or, do you need to ramp up gradually? Why? Then think about the implications of your success. How will reaching this goal affect the institution? Do you have the capacity to absorb these new students? If not, what will need to happen to support them? Remember, an incomplete answer is better than no answer at all.

4. What resources do we have available?

Resources aren't limited to the money in your budget. We've seen schools fail by not anticipating that increased spending on recruitment marketing will affect the staff charged with responding to new leads. The marketing budget might be available to push the number of leads generated through the roof, but if leads languish in a database of prospects to be contacted "someday," then yield will drop and everyone will wonder why the spiffy new advertising campaign — and bigger budget — didn't produce the desired results.

Even worse, prospects who haven't received the information they requested will have a negative perception of the institution. And that's an attitude they may be happy to share with peers on social networks.

Besides determining if you have enough staff, you should also factor in institutional resources such as hardware, software, and physical space. If your plan requires a new database, phone system, or access to additional facilities, can you get these resources when you need them? This can be tricky if you're beholden to other departments or a procurement process. If you don't have a guarantee that resources will be available when you need them, don't count them as "available" in your strategic plan.

5. Who are we trying to reach?

Start by classically defining your audiences using factors such as demographics, geography, and level of academic achievement. Once you get these factors down, you can move into more complex territory, including psychographic and sociological dimensions. Then, look at how context comes into play. Are there situational aspects that might impact who is more or less likely to choose your institution? Does a specific moment in the decision-making process affect how you reach out to your intended audience? Could external factors that don't fit into typical audience definitions make your target audience more or less appropriate for the new campaign? Are there any social, cultural, or economic trends that make your institution more or less attractive to a particular group? Are there any technological trends that impact these audiences and how you reach them? Finally, consider defining the "customer journeys" that lead to your institution. Typically, a prospect journey progresses through six phases:

1. **EXPLORATION:** Exploring potential schools and schooling options.

2. **AWARENESS:** When the prospect first becomes aware of your institution and adds them to their list.

3. **EVALUATION:** When the prospect refines their list of potential institutions to a shortlist they plan to apply to.

4. **APPLICATION:** Applying to the schools they've chosen.

5. **DECISION:** Evaluating admissions offers to make a final decision about where to enroll.

6. **ENROLLMENT:** The final stage of actually enrolling (and paying).

For each of these stages, try to define the following dimensions:

- **ACTIVITY:** What is the prospect doing at this stage of their journey?

- **CONCERNS:** What does the prospect worry about during this phase of their journey?

- **BARRIERS:** What might be holding them back from progressing to the next stage?

- **MESSAGING**: What kinds of messaging might they respond to during this phase? What will resonate? What will help alleviate their concerns and overcome their barriers?

- **CHANNELS**: What are the most effective channels for communicating with them during this phase? Typically, these start out broad and impersonal (broadcast, out-of-home, social, search) and become more focused as the journey progresses (text messaging, personalized emails, phone calls).

Depending on your target audience, adding dimensions such as influencers (e.g., parents and guidance counselors for undergraduate prospects) or even timing (due dates, testing dates) could help you form a more complete understanding of your target audiences.

If this sounds complex, don't worry. We devote a whole chapter to audience later in the book.

PROSPECT JOURNEY

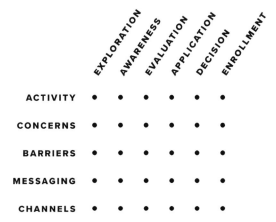

For a chart detailing each phase and dimension of the prospect journey, please visit nobodycares.idfive.com.

6. Why them?

Answering this question well requires breaking free from conventional wisdom. It's easy to get into a rut, going after the same prospective student pool every year. But if your yields start to decline, maybe it's time to look at different prospect groups to see how well they align with institutional priorities. Maybe you need to examine admissions standards to see how they fit with the demographic trends affecting your traditional pool. Or maybe you need to look for opportunities in groups traditionally underserved by your institution. The possibilities are endless, but no matter which groups you decide to pursue, you need to be able to answer why you're going after them and how your institution is a qualified candidate for their academic and professional plans.

7. If we do this, what are we going to do less of?

In our experience, no one has an unlimited budget. Doing something new often means doing less of something else. And this discussion usually has staffing implications. Reassigning or eliminating personnel — especially if you're going to replace them with new people that bring a different skill set — is never easy in higher ed. Take a hard look at places where you might duplicate efforts or would do so if you pursued a new strategy. If duplication happens, you may be able to shift resource allocations to get by. Next, examine your various existing initiatives by asking some hard questions. Why are you doing what you're doing? What are you (specifically) trying to accomplish? Is the effort succeeding? If not — or if you don't know because you can't measure performance — consider ending the initiative to do something new. It may seem risky, but it's not a good idea to continue wasting resources.

8. Which internal processes or politics will have an impact on what we're trying to do?

"Politics" and "processes" are often inextricably linked. Usually, things are done the way they are done because someone wants them done that way. The *safe* thing to do is to accept them and deal with the situation. The *right* thing to do is to take a hard look at what's going on and why. In some instances, you may find that you can't change what's going on. And that's OK. At least you've identified the problem. However, sometimes you *can* do something, especially if what's happening is under your direct area of responsibility. Either way, the key is to understand what's going on and what outcomes it's generating.

One of the most common ways politics and processes collide is when someone has been in a position long enough to serve as the "institutional memory." They are black boxes, taking inputs and producing outputs without anyone having any idea what they're doing to make decisions. And while it may have worked at one time, many of these people end up being bottlenecks or obstructions to progress. It's vital to your strategic planning to identify these "black boxes" and be honest about what impact these people, or units, are going to have on your efforts.

Additionally, take a hard look at how the processes and habits of other departments may affect your efforts. If the admissions team routinely ignores your requests for information about how and when they follow up on leads that you provide, you need to consider this in your planning and not count on receiving information from them. If graduate program recruitment happens at the department or program level, you are dependent upon the department chair or program director to follow up with prospects *and* provide you with some indication of how well your graduate recruitment initiatives are going. If they're not doing either, consider alternative methods to accomplish your goal. For example, if your information request forms go to the program director, send a copy to your office as well so you have some of the information you need. Also, ask friends and family to "secret shop" by sending in requests for information and then reporting to you on what they receive. It provides insight into the players, politics, and processes that are vital to your strategy.

9. Who's going to be in charge?

Understanding roles and responsibilities should be obvious, but it rarely is. If the person responsible for implementing your strategy isn't capable of making the decisions required to keep it on track — or if you can't figure out who that person should be — your plan is doomed to failure. While you often can't do anything to change who's in charge, knowing who that person is (or who those people are) will help you craft an executable strategy that's realistically designed to either distribute responsibility or alleviate the need for too much intervention.

In some instances, you may also need to account for someone who either doesn't agree with your strategy or has a competing (but unspoken) strategy. Again, you may not be able to do anything to change that person's role or influence, but you can account for the effect on what you're trying to accomplish.

As you work through these nine questions, remember that you and your team can't control every factor. Mitigate risk by answering each question as honestly and comprehensively as possible. Then revisit them throughout the life of your project to keep everyone on the same page.

Once your team has a shared vision — or is as close to one as you can muster — you're ready to gather information about the external factors you face.

Case Study:
Understanding Who You Are

It was a fun assignment: redesign the website of a private, faith-based, selective small college in the Southwest. We knew that doing the right thing would depend on us understanding the institution and its audiences in as much depth as possible.

We began with a multi-day visit to the campus, where our plan was to talk to administrators, faculty, staff, and students and, just as importantly, experience the school for ourselves. We wanted to gather answers for as many of the internal assessment questions as possible and answer additional questions we had, such as: What does it feel like to be on campus? What is it like to interact with the faculty, staff, and students? What sets the institution apart? Why do people decide to attend the school?

One of the most lasting images — and the one that helped us understand the people of the institution better than anything else — was the wall of backpacks lining the entrance to the cafeteria. The backpacks, hanging from hooks and sitting on the floor, were unattended. They awaited their owners to retrieve them before going back to class.

It was a small detail, but these backpacks represented the perfect distillation of the sense of trust, openness, and community that permeated the campus.

Even though many people on the outside perceived the school to be a conservative institution, we discovered through our interviews and casual conversations that the school prided itself on intellectual inquiry and rigorous academics. It was founded on a "great books" model with a core curriculum shared by all undergraduates, an approach that led to a level of community and shared purpose that we'd rarely seen anywhere else. Thanks to this sense of community, the faculty, students, staff, and administration were unified in their commitment to intellectual inquiry, rigorous thought, and a mission to serve the world.

Using the brand attributes our assessment uncovered, we developed a marketing strategy — and ultimately designed a website — focused on communicating the same sense of joy, wonder, and, to be honest, surprise that we experienced on campus. The project taught us that, when you take the time to ask plenty of questions, insight can come from unexpected places. Even from unattended backpacks.

THE FORCES: UNDERSTANDING YOUR INITIAL CONDITIONS

35

If you're going to create something that gets you the results you need, you first have to understand the institutional environmental factors you face. In the OpenEDU Model, we call these environmental factors "forces" and focus on the four most important ones:

- **BUDGET:** How much money do you have to work with?

- **TIME:** How much time do you have to work with? And at what time of year will you deploy your plan?

- **GOALS:** What do you want to accomplish?

- **BRAND PERCEPTION:** How does your audience's perceptions of your institution differ from what you want them to perceive?

The First Force: Budget

Budgets are destiny. They impact everything you do because they dictate what you can afford. There is no use in engineering a regional branding campaign that includes expensive out-of-home, radio, and television tactics if your budget only supports a couple of print ads in the local newspaper's educational supplement.

That said, it's wrong to think of budgets as lists of expenses. What you do to market your institution in order to increase awareness and drive enrollments is an investment in the future of your institution. Sure, marketing plans require money up front, but if you do your job correctly, return on investment will be many multiples of what you spent.

We think this bears repeating: *Marketing expenses are investments, not costs.* Pitching your budget as an investment rather than a cost can help leadership loosen their death grip on the budget. This approach may also buy you patience and time, which are requirements for all great investments to mature and pay significant returns.

You'll need to plan for two primary investments: professional services and media. Professional services include research, strategy, creative, production, media buying, reporting, and ongoing support. Your media investments will cover the advertisement placements if your plan includes paid media. But not all plans include paid media. For example, you might focus efforts on earned media, such as organic social media, search engine optimization, public relations, and grassroots outreach. Nevertheless, just because you're not paying for media doesn't mean it's free. Even unpaid media efforts require people's time. When budgeting, consider your human resources too.

Most often, media is the biggest investment in a plan. Savvy partners will negotiate great media rates and added-value on your behalf. And while it might have been the norm in the past for the folks planning and buying your media to take a commission on the value of that media, that isn't the case anymore. Insist that your partners don't charge a commission. A fee-for-services approach is a lot more honest (and transparent).

Budgets vary widely across institutions. Corporations looking to retain their current market position should put about 5% of their gross revenue toward marketing. Businesses that are looking to grow or gain market share should put 10% or more of their gross revenue toward marketing.

However, most colleges and universities can't afford marketing budgets at a corporate level. While well-funded schools typically have $3 million to $5 million in their annual marketing budgets, many schools can make magic with budgets ranging from $500,000 to $1 million.

When your budget is limited, your best bet is to go digital, focusing and staggering your buys. Digital media is more economical than traditional media, it allows you to hyper-target sophisticated segments, and it can drive more action than traditional media in the short-term.

So, let's look at an example of how to put together a budget. For reference, the sample spreadsheet detailing our budget can be found on page 40.

In our example, we're promoting a new part-time/evening master's in business program for a hypothetical bricks-and-mortar university. In future chapters, we'll take an in-depth look at how to determine your audience and reach them successfully. For now, it's enough to know that our audience lives in the area and will be predominantly made up of mid-career professionals.

To reach this audience and move them from initial interest to enrollment, we'll need to invest in a number of marketing initiatives. After much consideration (again, we'll go into the finer points of creating a campaign later on), we determine that we should purchase search ads on Google, radio spots on NPR, and display ads in the local paper's print and online editions. These ads will direct people to a landing page that provides additional information about the program and features a form that allows prospects to request more information. In addition, we'll host two open houses that will be promoted through some of the ad buy and through a direct mailer sent to anyone who has expressed interest in the program. Finally, we'll produce a brochure, which we can hand out at the open houses or mail to prospects who can't attend but have requested more information.

To see how the costs of this plan break out, review the sample budget on page 40. While $250,000 might seem like a lot, most people spend a long time deciding whether to pursue a graduate degree. As such, the campaign has to build awareness throughout that extended decision-making process while also generating leads through more direct-response tactics. This budget covers a year's worth of smart, targeted efforts that should generate plenty of high-value leads.

SAMPLE MARKETING BUDGET

Total investment available:	$250,000.00		
		COST PER DAY	DAYS
Google AdWords	$67,500.00	$375.00	
NPR Local Sponsorship	$5,000.00		
Daily Newspaper Online	$3,600.00	$20.00	
Daily Newspaper Print	$26,100.00	$290.00	
Total Media Spend	**$102,200.00**		
Open Houses (2)	**$10,000.00**		
		COST EACH #	PRINTED
Open House Postcard 1	$75.00	$0.05	1,500
Open House Postcard 2	$100.00	$0.05	2,000
Fall mailing	$500.00	$0.25	2,000
Spring mailing	$750.00	$0.30	2,500
Program brochures	$225.00	$0.15	1,500
Total Printing	**$1,650.00**		
Postage	**$2,240.00**		
Campaign landing page	**$15,000.00**		
New program website	**$35,000.00**		
		PER MONTH	MONTHS
SEO Services	**$18,000.00**	**$1,500.00**	12
Creative Services	**$39,000.00**	**$3,250.00**	12
Contingency Fund	**$25,000.00**		
Total 12 Mo. Expenditures	**$248,090.00**		

Of course, our example budget covers just one scenario. You might want to focus your marketing on promoting specific programs that perform well traditionally and have "infinite" operational capacity, or you might want to highlight older programs that are struggling. There are plenty of viable ways to spend your budget, just avoid spreading it too thin by marketing everything all at once. Focusing your budget isn't a politically popular strategy at most universities, but it's the only one that makes sense. If you get pushback from smaller programs that feel they're being left out, you may want to gently point out that office and classroom facilities on campus are not allocated equally to each program either.

Pro tip: Squirrel away 10% to 15% of your budget. Sometimes projects run hot and you'll need the extra resources to keep the campaign running. However, make sure that you're familiar with your institution's policies about money that's left over at the end of the fiscal year. If you're in a "use it or lose it" situation, it doesn't make sense to leave money on the table. If you can't figure out how to spend it, you may want to consult your finance folks for creative (and above-board) ways to keep the money in your budget for later use.

Case Study:
Counting Pennies

After presenting the outcome of the OpenEDU Model at the American Marketing Association's annual Symposium for the Marketing of Higher Education, an elite university in the Northeast asked if we could help market some of their programs. We said, "Sure."

The school was intrigued by our success with email marketing strategies that generate request for information (RFI) submissions. We reviewed their enrollment goals and timeline. We also looked at the programs in question, the challenges the programs faced, and their traffic, destination, and nurture strategy.

We recommended focusing most of the limited budget and time on an email campaign. By using specific email lists, we can typically cut out a year of the lead-to-enrollment cycle by reaching a targeted audience that is further along in the decision-making process.

We drafted a series of emails for each of the programs and used URLs with tracking. To help drive leads, we included offer codes waiving the application fee.

We designed our landing pages to collect leads for the primary programs we were marketing first. Upon submission of the inquiry form, a confirmation page suggested other, similar programs worth considering in the graduate school. The campaign yielded direct enrollments thanks to the application fee waiver code and information on related programs.

We saw a 23% lead-to-started/completed application rate within the first six months of the overall campaign. In fact, some programs saw 31% of all form submissions resulting in applications.

The Second Force: Time

When thinking about how to deploy your resources, it's important to think beyond the notion that "resources" only equals "money." Time is a resource as well and its value is measured in opportunity.

Your campaigns will have three timelines:

1. Research/planning so you can understand your audiences and plan how you intend to reach them
2. Creative development, including testing
3. The media flight itself

Depending on how much primary research is necessary, the research and planning phase can take anywhere from one to four months. Once research and planning is complete, you can start creative.

Creative development may be fast or slow, since it's a subjective process. The number of creative deliverables and the approval process that often includes multiple administrative (and sometimes academic) units can significantly slow the creative phase. But, we've found that the stronger the research, the easier it is to move through creative because research reduces subjectivity. When you have to go toe-to-toe with an influential advisory committee member (or your boss) who objects to a certain creative approach, it helps to show that your actual research with actual prospective undergraduates demonstrated that the campaign resonates well with the particular target audience. Strong research is a great way to overcome objections and gently remind the person who is objecting that they're *really* not the target market.

A high degree of collaboration between the creative and business teams also helps move creative development forward. Make sure you have a strong creative brief that's substantiated by the research, schedule collaborative sessions where creative and business viewpoints can be aired, are honest with your feedback, keep the lines of communication open at all times, and test concepts with target audiences (if you have the budget) to make sure that every creative decision is backed up with real-world data. If everyone acts on good faith, relies on research, and communicates with each other, the outcome will invariably be something you can all be proud of.

Finally, make sure you build in production time when creating your project timelines. It might take two to four weeks to conceive, create, and produce a straightforward display banner campaign for a single program, provided there is good research, available photography assets, and a minimal approval process. The creative for a comprehensive integrated advertising campaign that includes radio, billboard, display advertising, search engine marketing, social media marketing, email, and out-of-home advertising could take anywhere from two to four months.

Doing good work takes time. From start to finish, you could spend as much as six months before you're able to launch your campaign. But, as we pointed out earlier, time is just as much of an investment as money. It's always better to spend more time to do it right, as long as that time is spent wisely.

Pro tip: Get into a routine. Schedule a standing daily, weekly, or biweekly meeting with all parties involved to align, prioritize, and commiserate. It doesn't matter when you decide to have your call; what matters is that you make it a habit. Even if all you have to talk about is the weather, the discipline is healthy for the project and it will keep everyone on track.

Case Study: Time Matters

When a small public university in the Midwest contacted us, they wanted a quick campaign. Previous attempts at reaching out to prospective undergrads had fallen short, and they were worried they weren't going to reach their goals. Worst of all, they were running out of time. The recruitment season was well underway.

Obviously, the need was urgent. But we didn't realize how urgent until they told us we only had a few weeks to get a campaign up and running. We made it happen because they were willing to collaborate closely with us in order to make the best use of the time we had. We both knew we were running out of time and the work took priority for everyone involved.

We had to prioritize. We worked together to identify the programs that would yield the best results, the audiences that were most likely to respond, and the message that would resonate with those audiences and drive them to take action as quickly as possible. Then, we identified the elements of their brand experience that would spur action and collaborated to brainstorm creative approaches that would get us the results we wanted.

The client arranged a photo shoot featuring actual students and we developed the creative assets we needed in one day. With a strong brand platform for our work, we were able to quickly transform those elements into action-oriented ads that could be deployed across both digital and print platforms. The results exceeded expectations. Even though we worked fast, we never lost sight of the core elements: brand and audience.

The Third Force: Goals

Let's be clear: Goals are not strategy. Goals exist before strategy and they stay the same throughout the entire process of developing a marketing campaign. That's why we consider them one of the forces bearing down on everything you do. Your decisions, from initial research to deployment of nurture tactics, have to account for the goals.

However, unlike with budgets or with time, you have significant control over your goals. Even if others in your institution will be playing a role in setting them, you'll (hopefully) have a seat at that table. And having a seat — and a say — can help you ensure that your team follows a smart goal-setting process that keeps goals simple and explicit.

One great method for running the goal-setting process is to use a kind of Madlibs-like device that forces everyone to be precise. At the start of your campaign planning, have everyone attending the meeting complete the following sentence:

We want to (specific, measurable change) **among** (audience segment/s) **in order to** (specific, measurable outcome) **because** (reason for campaign).

It might be a short sentence, but there's a lot packed in there:

- **A specific, measurable change that will lead to the outcome you want.** Being precise here helps you and your team *really* think about what you want. Writing "increase applications" makes a lot more sense here than "increase traffic to the website."

- **The specific audience segment or segments that you hope to influence and attract.** Again, precision is important here. "Everybody" is *never* the answer to "Who are we trying to reach?"

- **The specific, measurable outcome you want to achieve.** It could theoretically be anything, but it must relate directly to the change you've already specified. Think about the ultimate reason why you want to create change. For example, it's OK to say that you want your campaign to increase applications, but the outcome you choose makes all the difference. A campaign to increase applications in order to boost your selectivity numbers is a lot different than a campaign to increase enrollment in a flagging graduate program.

- **An explicitly stated "why."** Understanding — and being honest about — why you're about to commit a bunch of resources to a project is vital to maintaining focus on your goals.

Be clear and precise about what you're trying to accomplish, but also realize there aren't any inherently "right" or "wrong" answers here. There's nothing wrong with saying "**We want to** increase traffic to our website **among** all audiences **in order to** keep the president happy because she likes seeing a lot of web traffic in her weekly reports," as long as everyone's clear on the goal as stated.

Goals can be accomplished *in sequence* (i.e. one after the other) or *in parallel* (several at the same time). For example, it's not unusual to want to promote specific programs while building awareness for the institution as a whole.

This kind of approach clears the way for the subsequent program-specific marketing with goals such as:

- Over a 6-month period, increase local (define local) awareness by 15% among undergraduate prospects, as measured by an awareness study.

- Once awareness is on the way up, work to increase qualified leads for a specific undergraduate program by 50% over the next few months, as measured by leads year-over-year during the corresponding period.

These are sequenced goals. Parallel goals have similar properties, but they run concurrently.

There are many ways to set marketing goals, but no matter how you approach setting your goals, make sure they're realistic, well articulated, adequately funded, and properly timed. If your goal is longer than one sentence and doesn't roll off the tip of your tongue, rethink it. You'll be glad you did when you're able to keep everyone focused on that shared vision.

Case Study:
Point & Follow

You've probably never heard of thanatology. Most people haven't. And that was our challenge.

A large public institution with a well-respected professional graduate program approached us with a well-defined goal: recruit 12 students into their new thanatology graduate certificate program.

First, thanatology wasn't exactly an easy sell. Defined as "the scientific study of death and the practices associated with it, including the study of the needs of the terminally ill and their families," it's a discipline that few would consider mainstream.

Nevertheless, we knew that there had to be a market. We just had to find it. And our client's focus on a specific goal, coupled with their knowledge of the market, made filling this new program a lot easier than it would have been if everything hadn't been clearly defined. In the end, we created a brand platform rooted in caring and compassion during death and dying. Then, we targeted audiences involved in professions that deal with those life stages and built a media plan that focused on paid search emphasizing keywords such as "nursing home jobs," "hospice," etc. Within the first six weeks, we delivered 80 leads from our search campaigns at a cost of just over $41 per lead.

Our client contacted every lead by phone the moment they came in. As a result, we got regular feedback related to the high quality of the leads generated. When the program was over, we'd recruited the 12 students the institution needed. It wasn't easy, but without a clearly defined goal, it would have been a lot more difficult.

How Structured Flexibility Can Help You Reach Your Goals

Have you ever spent time crafting the most elaborate and logical project plan you possibly could, taking every last detail into account? Did the plan feel unsinkable? And did it ultimately wash under the wave of unexpected complications and events?

In our experience, the most intricately designed project plans are the first to fall apart and the last to lead a project to its goal.

More of an attitude than a process, structured flexibility is designed to combat the kind of task-focused linear thinking that inevitably leads to tunnel vision and difficulty in reaching goals. We don't think saying, "It's always been done that way," is helpful. Instead, we approach projects based on the work of the two professions that best understand the futility (and arrogance) of assuming we can foresee everything in advance: the military and improvisational theater.

At West Point, soldiers learn a concept called "Commander's Intent." In this concept, high-ranking officers articulate high-level objectives (the *what*) to soldiers on the ground who are responsible for accomplishing these goals (the *how*). For example, if ordered to "take that hill," the junior officers on the ground can consider conditions that may have changed since the original assault plan was developed. If the officers want to take a new route that allows them to flank the enemy in order to complete the objective, they have the authority to do that. The key idea is that the plan isn't the goal — the goal is the goal. Adhering to the first plan simply because it was the first plan (or because it was *your* plan) makes it difficult if not impossible to react to changing realities. We believe in staying focused on the *what* while leaving space for the *how* to change as needed.

And that's where improvisational theater comes in. Improvisational actors know change well. By definition, they improvise dialogue and scenes based on uncertain conditions, such as audience input, scene changes, or other environmental factors. However, improvisation doesn't mean anarchy. Instead, people doing improv adhere to one simple rule: "Yes, and…" rule.

Responding to unexpected changes with a "Yes, and…" mindset forces actors to accept what's going on and then develop solutions on the fly that allow them to advance the discourse positively and intelligently.

A mountain of work has been done on the psychology and physiology of positivity and, at the risk of sounding way flakier than we are, we've seen amazing, productive, collaborative results with our clients and partners by using this technique.

When someone says, "Yes, and…," they will collaborate on a solution. It's the opposite of responding to changes with, "No, that's not what we agreed on." "Yes, and…" prompts solutions. "No" draws lines in the sand that someone must cross if the project is going to move forward. And "no" inevitably leads to hurt feelings, damaged relationships, and unmet goals.

The Fourth Force: Brand Perception

In the OpenEDU Model, "brand perception" is the fourth force
that influences what you ultimately create. "But my brand is my
foundation," you might be saying. And you're right. The brand
you want your institution to have *is* your foundation. But how
your brand is perceived by the outside world is a force you'll have
to contend with.

When it comes to your marketing efforts, it's important to understand
what happens when your institution comes into contact with its
audiences. Do they perceive you the way you want them to? Or do
they have a different idea of who you are and what you're about?

If there's a gap between your intended brand platform and the way
your brand is perceived, you have a problem. The experience of a brand
is a lot more powerful than the presentation of a brand. Trying to
present your brand in a way that's counter to your audience's experience
of it will make your marketing seem disingenuous, or at least irrelevant.

That's why research is so important and why we've devoted the entire
next chapter to it. Only through research can you discover if what your
audience feels about your brand is different than what you want them
to feel. If your brand platform and your audience's brand perception
are aligned, then you simply have to maintain that alignment. If there's
a gap, then you have to account for it.

How can you account for it? The first step is recognizing that you
can't simply broadcast your brand platform at a louder volume and
hope to change perceptions. For instance, a maker of cheap, poor-quality
beauty products may be able to temporarily boost sales by hiring a
beautiful celebrity spokesperson to attest to the products' quality but,
ultimately, the audience will figure out that the products are inferior and
respond accordingly.

To properly address a brand disconnect, you have to either change the brand experience or change the way you're presenting the brand. In the case of the beauty product company, they could improve their quality or they could shift marketing tactics — and the brand platform — to focus on areas that better fit their products, such as low cost and availability.

When Domino's Pizza realized they had a brand disconnect in the early 2010s, they responded with a campaign that pointed out that people thought their pizza was bad and paired that with the promotion of new (and improved!) crust and toppings. They also put a lot of money into going high-tech with their systems, correctly recognizing that their brand platform wasn't just pizza, but was pizza delivery. If they could deliver good-enough pizza in a fast and efficient way, they knew they could realign brand perception to meet their brand platform. And it worked.[4] By the end of 2016, Domino's was the second-largest pizza chain in the world and its stock had risen from $8.76 a share to nearly $160 a share.

In a perfect world, how people perceive us and how we want them to perceive us would be one and the same. But the reality is, those two aspects of branding are sometimes at odds. And your marketing campaign will need to adjust for that as much as it adjusts for your budget, goals, and time constraints.

Case Study:
A Tricky Thing

A brand is a tricky thing. Every institution has one (whether they like it or not), but it is often difficult to define in a way that's true to the values of the institution and appeals to those who don't know the school. This is especially true if a school's core values might lead to preconceived notions.

We faced this challenge when working with a small, private, Catholic college in the upper Midwest. The institution had existed for more than a hundred years, and we knew that people who were unfamiliar with the brand might be turned off by the school's religious affiliation and perceived values. It was our job to figure out how to remain true to the college's brand and mission while creating a brand experience that appealed to a wider range of prospective students.

To do so, we had to get to the core of who they are. We interviewed leadership, administrators, faculty, and students in order to better understand the campus experience. We examined the content on their site and what they sent out to prospective students. And we researched what kinds of values might appeal to prospects. Then, we sat down to think.

Rather than couching the brand with language that screamed "Catholic," we were able to distill the brand down into three words that spoke to the values of the institution in a way that resonated with their heritage and appealed to the interests of today's prospective students. Those few short words spoke to a wide range of hopefuls and helped enhance the college's brand.

—

There are many ways to set marketing goals, but no matter how you approach setting your goals, make sure they're realistic, well-articulated, adequately funded, and properly timed.

To create a successful marketing campaign, you have to know your audience and their motivations. Today's prospective college students are shaped by ever-changing and often elusive market, social, and technological forces, meaning the prospective student you're talking to today is not the same as the one you spoke to five or ten years ago. So, how can you figure out the best ways to reach and influence them? The answer is research.

A Crash Course in Research

Start with a Research Strategy

Effective research begins and ends with a good research strategy. You need to be clear about your research goals and how the data you gather will be used; and you need to plan carefully and select methods appropriate to what you need to find out. If you just go into a research project with a half-baked idea of what you want and no clear strategy for getting it, you'll just be wasting time and money.

As we discussed in our introduction, a strategy doesn't have to be complicated. It's just about creating an approach to solving a problem. However, as we also discussed, a good strategy needs to be based on a thorough understanding of the problem you're trying to solve. A clearly defined strategy can serve as a benchmark to evaluate every decision related to your research.

There are five dimensions to consider when creating a research strategy:

- **PROBLEM**: What's the problem you're trying to solve? Why does it need to be resolved?

- **OUTPUT**: What are you planning to create that you hope your research will inform? Whether it's a website, an ad, a brochure, or the strategic underpinnings for a far reaching marketing campaign, it's important to agree on what you will, in the end, produce.

- **AUDIENCE**: Who are you hoping will see or use what you're making? It's vital to define whom you're creating for — and why.

- **MARKET**: What's the context for what you're doing? What are the external forces at work? Who are your competitors?

- **INTERNAL SITUATION**: What forces are at work within the institution? What processes and procedures are impacted? What institutional roadblocks might stand in the way?

Some of these questions might be difficult to answer until after you've completed your research (e.g., your understanding of your audience may change once your research into the audience is complete). That's OK. The point is to go in with a clearly defined purpose. From there, you can put together a plan for executing your research strategy. For that plan, we recommend following these four steps.

1. **DEFINE THE PROBLEM**

2. **DEFINE THE DESIRED OUTCOME(S)**

3. **DEFINE WHAT YOU'RE TRYING TO MEASURE (AND WHY YOU WANT TO MEASURE IT)**

4. **DEFINE HOW YOU'RE GOING TO COLLECT DATA**

These steps take a deductive approach, moving from the big picture (understanding the problem) to the specific (measurement and methods). We find this is a useful technique for projects with a limited scope, such as testing a hypothesis or solving a specific problem.

An inductive approach — going from specific observations to general observations/theories/hypotheses — often requires additional time, effort, and money. (For instance, conducting a field ethnography to form theories about the behavior of specific groups is a major undertaking.) It doesn't mean an inductive approach is useless; just beware that it can become unwieldy.

When crafting a research agenda that will use a deductive approach, it's often useful to summarize the four steps in a simple document to ensure that everyone is, literally, on the same page. Here's an example:

What problem are we trying to solve?	Declining enrollments in our graduate programs.
What kind of outcome(s) do we hope to achieve with this research project?	A better understanding of the external forces/trends that might have an impact on graduate admission for our institution (and our peers).
What does our research need to measure for us to better understand this problem?	Recent enrollment trends (within two years) in similar programs.
How are we going to collect the data we need and why are those methods going to be best?	A review of third-party research seems to be the most cost-effective way to resolve the issue. We'll pay particular attention to reliable third-party sources, most likley government information providers.

Getting the Data You Need

Once you've decided what you're trying to learn with your research, you have to figure out how you're going to get that information. Doing this properly requires a research method.

You can choose from a broad range of research methods, including one-on-one interviews, focus groups, surveys, and reviews of third-party research. The right tool varies. Some research methods are excellent at obtaining big-picture data about subjects that are tough to quantify (e.g., focus groups are good at giving impressions about design). Others are good at delivering narrowly focused data from large groups (surveys work well for this). The method(s) you choose depends on what kind of data you require to develop your strategy, your available resources, and the accessible populations.

Sampling

Unless you have a considerable budget or a narrow research topic (e.g., "The Attitudes and Opinions of Institution X's Geography Faculty About the Recent Departure of the Department Chair"), you can only reach out to a subset of your audience. That's OK. It's still possible to draw useful conclusions from a representative sample.

Resources for the statistically challenged

"Marketing Analysis: Unlocking The Power Of Descriptive Statistics"[5] — Excellent short intro to fundamental concepts such as statistical significance, standard deviation, etc., and how marketers can use them.

Discovering Statistics[6] — Resources, tutorials, and other tools to help you get a grip on everything from basic statistical calculations to some of the more important advanced concepts.

How to Lie With Statistics[7]— Even though it was written in 1954 this (now) free ebook is as relevant today as it was more than half a century ago — maybe even more so. It does a great job entertainingly and irreverently explaining how statistics can be used to bend or obscure the truth. Sure, you could use these tricks if you're evil, but we hope you use what you learn to be a better truth-teller and a more critical thinker.

How many people constitute a sample? If you ask a statistician, prepare yourself for a lecture on "statistical significance." Ask someone who conducts usability testing and they'll tell you that fewer than 10 (usually seven) will suffice.

In practice, the ideal sample size depends on a combination of resources and needs. A discussion about calculating statistical significance is outside the scope of this book, but we're willing to risk the ire of statisticians everywhere by saying the practical answer is usually "enough to feel right." Generally speaking, you can get a feel for what seems to work based on your experience and industry benchmarks. When in doubt, a quick trip to Google to seek out studies that are similar to yours should inform your target sample size.

To choose your sample, use one of these common methods.

- **CONVENIENCE:** i.e., "Who can we get in the time we have for the money we want to spend?" If you don't have a database of research subjects, recruiting subjects will depend on human factors such as availability, proximity, and attention. And you're usually stuck with whomever you can get.

- **RANDOM SAMPLE:** If you have access to a pool of potential subjects, use a randomization method to get a useful sample.

- **SYSTEMATIC:** Begin with a random selection as a starting point in your potential research subject pool. Then, use a systematic method to choose other subjects (e.g., every fifth person on a list after the randomly selected subject).

- **STRATIFIED SAMPLING:** Used most frequently when you have to be sure that all members of a particular group (e.g., a political affiliation) are represented in the final research sample.

- **CLUSTER SAMPLING:** Similar to stratified sampling, this is useful when you have to develop a sample that includes a subset of the population with a particular characteristic (e.g., prospective undergraduates living in rural counties in a state with 10 rural counties), choosing a subset of this group (five of the 10 possible counties), and then testing everyone who matches the criteria in the selected subgroup.

There are many issues surrounding sampling. They can (and do) fill the pages of many textbooks. However, you should at least be aware of the issues that make developing a representative sample — or, at least, what feels like a representative sample — difficult:

- **MISSING ELEMENTS**: You can't find the people you're looking for in your database or you can't locate them using recruiting techniques. You could go back and try to cast a wider net, but, if you can't find the subjects that work for you, you may want to reconsider your research question.

- **FOREIGN ELEMENTS**: You end up with members of your sample who don't belong there. This can occur for many reasons, including incorrect data collection, deliberate misrepresentation by research subjects, or unclear recruiting instructions.

- **DUPLICATE ELEMENTS**: It's not uncommon for people to show up more than once in a database. Make sure to scrub your database of duplicates before you start.

Research Methods

Once you've decided whom you're going to look at in your research, you have to determine the method you'll use to get the data you need. Which method is right for you? It depends on whom (or what) you have access to, your resources, and what you're looking for.

Here are some of the most common research methods used by marketing and communications professionals.

Surveys

Surveys are one of the most useful methods for gathering data about the behavior, attitudes, opinions, and experiences of a sample of a particular population. Typically, surveys are administered systematically, often providing the subjects with multiple-choice questions.

Surveys have the advantage of being easily administered to a large number of subjects, particularly when they're conducted remotely, such as over the telephone, online via email or social media, or on paper through the mail. However, the breadth and quality of the questions included in the survey dictate limitations.

If you're interested in using surveys in your research (and you don't possess an advanced degree in statistics and market research), we urge you to seek out the services of a competent, experienced market research professional. They may cost more upfront, but when it comes to yielding beneficial results, it's a worthwhile investment to pay someone who knows what they're doing.

CAUTION: While we don't have the space to take a deep-dive into survey design, please remember to avoid too many open-ended, fill-in-the-blank questions. It may be tempting to try to gather more nuanced qualitative data, but we can assure you that it's not going to work. These types of questions are incredibly challenging and time-consuming to analyze. And, if you administer your survey in a self-service remote format (e.g., online), a good number of participants won't answer them.

One-on-One Interviews

Researchers sit down (either in person or remotely) with a list of questions or a discussion guide that serves as a touchstone for the conversation. One-on-one interviews are useful for situations where you have:

1. A small sample size.

2. Important individuals who can offer significant information but need to recuse themselves from larger group discussions to avoid influencing opinions (e.g., people in leadership roles).

Facilitated Discussion Groups

If you have a large number of people to hear from, or if you want to gather multiple perspectives on a particular topic, a group discussion is incredibly useful. However, you have to be careful to assemble a representative sample of the group you're researching and be aware that people often behave differently in groups than they do when participating in a one-on-one session. We always find it helpful to assure discussion group members that their answers will remain anonymous and that we'll avoid using direct quotes in our final report. Remember: College campuses are small places.

Focus Groups

Unlike with facilitated group discussions, a focus group uses a moderator to guide the conversation around a particular set of questions. We find this rigid, systematic methodology to be a lot less useful than a well-moderated, flexible discussion group.

Observation/Ethnography

Observing research subjects in their natural environments is a type of qualitative research designed to gather data about subjects without direct intervention. This method can yield some valuable data, but it's important to recognize a few issues:

- Subjects who are aware they're under observation may behave differently than they otherwise would. Unless you take great care to hide yourself, your presence will likely skew the results.

- Observational research is a more inductive approach that can take a long time to yield the information you want, if it yields anything at all.

- To be truly effective, observers should receive training on both observation and data recording before going in the field.

Historical

Sometimes, it's useful to eschew live subjects for the historical record. This type of research can be beneficial when it comes to providing context, and it has the added benefit of not having to deal with the idiosyncrasies of live human beings.

Case Studies

Researching case studies created by others (or studying your prior case studies) is a good way of providing a broad context that ranges across multiple institutions, situations, or initiatives.

Those are the basics of qualitative research. While we probably haven't provided enough to make you into a market researcher, we hope that you have sufficient information to appreciate why research is so crucial in the development of your marketing strategies.

Case Study:
Survey Surprise!

Research can help you gain the kind of understanding you need to develop a marketing/communications plan that works. But, it can also be a marketing tool.

A respected business school came to us with a simple question: Why are we having a hard time recruiting students for our executive education program? Executive education programs are pricey and they're often paid for by companies interested in professional development. To find out why more companies weren't taking advantage of our client's tremendous offerings, we had to get to those who held the purse strings: human resources directors.

We crafted two surveys. One went to potential executive ed students and the other went to HR directors at their companies. The survey, sent via LinkedIn InMail, was relatively brief and asked: What can you tell us about your reimbursement policies for professional development? We also tacked on one final question: Can we contact you about programs that you're offering?

The results exceeded everyone's expectations, with a response rate that was over 40% for both groups. It turned out that large companies were most likely to pay for professional development. And they wanted some precise training, mostly centered around technology and leadership.

By the end, we had two things: great insights into what our local audiences wanted and a whole bunch of leads representing HR directors who wanted to know more about the program.

DEFINING YOUR AUDIENCES

67

After you've done your initial research, you should have a better idea of who it is you should be talking to and who might be influencing their decision about where/if they'll attend school. However, transforming those insights into an understanding of your audience takes a few more steps. And those steps start with one truth:

You can't effectively market to everyone.

If you take away only one thing from this chapter, let that be it. Effectively reaching everyone with your marketing would take an unlimited budget. And if you have that, please stop reading and call us now.

Unfortunately, unlimited budgets are a fantasy. In the real world, budget constraints and a need for ROI require us to tailor our marketing messages to the audiences who will have the most impact on the buying decision. And we have to reach those audiences through the media that they're most likely to be using at the moments they'll be most receptive to our message.

The best way to accomplish this is to have well-defined audience segments based on in-depth understandings, not broad assumptions. While it's easy to say, "Well, we've always done things this way" — especially if how your institution has always done things has been working (more or less) up to now — you're doing little more than relying on luck and fickle intuition. In a world where technology is constantly overturning assumptions about who our audiences are, what influences their decisions, and how they behave, you need data if you want to be successful.

Where can you find that data? Your research will uncover a lot of it. To provide you with even more, we've compiled data on multiple aspects of modern audiences and their habits. Following that, we'll guide you through the process of clearly defining your audiences.

Attention in the Multi-Screen Universe

Today's audiences can get their information and entertainment in a lot of ways. That's obvious to everyone. But dealing with the realities of today's multi-screen media universe is not always easy. To handle the modern media environment, we first have to get over some pervasive preconceptions about how media works.

When it comes to advertising, most of us have been brought up to think of "media" as being comprised of several totally separate realms. At the highest level, there's "traditional" versus "digital" media. Dig down into traditional and it's typically divided into television, print, out-of-home, and radio, which are considered mass media platforms. Digital is a little more complicated, but we can start with mobile app versus website and then break each into smaller pieces based on format: display, search, in-app, etc.

Considering how we divide things — and, to be fair, we're often forced to, based on how media is bought and sold — it would be easy to think that each medium and format within that medium exists on its own. Television is separate from radio. Search is separate from online display advertising (e.g. banner ads). Mobile display advertising is different than streaming video advertising, etc. But, in today's media universe, thinking in terms of divisions is dead wrong. Thanks to recent technological advancements — and the ways we think about those advancements — we're in a whole new media universe.

The Rise and Fall of Convergence

Two things occurred that ushered us into the new media age. The first step was the digitization of nearly everything, which was a consequence of the mass adoption of the internet and the World Wide Web. Tim Berners-Lee invented the web because he was looking for an easier way to share scientific papers with his colleagues at the European Organization for Nuclear Research. As usage increased, people began to realize that they could use the web to publish original content, and publishers discovered another channel for what they printed.

Innovative people quickly realized that the web could serve as a publishing platform for *anything* digital. Video, music, games, animation, and other digital content started to appear. While technology and bandwidth initially limited the spread of digital content, early visionaries saw the potential and ran with it. In fact, Pseudo.com, the world's first online television network, was founded in 1993 and attracted millions of users before going down in flames during the dot-com bust of 2000. (Check out the excellent documentary *We Live in Public*[8] to learn more about Pseudo.)

Over time, we began to understand the web as a *meta-medium*, delivering everything that all traditional media offered and doing so in one place. From this came the theory of *convergence*, the expectation that TV and computers would merge, letting us live happily with one big screen in the living room that gave us all the content we could consume.

But a funny thing happened. New types of screens started to pop up, allowing us to access content over the internet in a way that didn't feel like using a computer *or* watching a television. These screens were a lot smaller, more portable, and more *personal*.

First, smartphones let us access internet content anytime and anyplace we had a cellular signal. Then came tablets. Not the wonky personal digital assistants of the late 90's (remember the Palm Pilot?) or the clunky tablet PCs of the early 2000's, but thin devices with relatively large screens and long battery life (compared to laptops). They allowed us to curl up with e-books in a way that approximated a print book, surf the web from the couch or the bed without overheating laptop batteries burning our legs, and play games just by touching the screen. They turned on instantly, ran for hours, and were so easy to use that a baby could use one. Heck, there are even iPad games designed for *cats*.[9]

Instead of one-screen convergence, we've arrived at something very different: multiple screens that disconnect content from the limitations of time and space and allow us to access it in a very personal way. What we once had to consume on a TV, over the radio, on a computer at our desks, on a CD player, or through a DVD player is now available on a bus, on a couch, or from the beach. Modern technology has freed us from the traditional constraints and divorced media from its eponymous containers. We can even consume multiple types of media simultaneously on multiple devices — a reality that's having a bigger impact on marketing than you might think.

Through the Rabbit Hole

The first symptom that times were changing was when younger people — usually the earliest adopters of new technology — began cutting down on their television consumption. According to aggregated viewer data from Nielsen, in the first quarter of 2015, 18- to 24-year-olds watched an average of 18 hours and four minutes of television per week.[10] By the third quarter of 2018, that number had dropped to 12 hours and 57 minutes, a reduction of nearly 30%. All other age groups now show similar — if less precipitous — declines in TV viewership.

Where's that TV time going? According to recent research published by eMarketer, our attention is being directed to digital devices.[11] In fact, according to their study, consumers spend almost twice as much time per day with digital devices (six hours and 35 minutes) than watching television (three hours and 35 minutes).

But the really profound change is that we're spending our time using all these screens simultaneously. According to Nielsen, 45% of U.S. adults report using a digital device "always" or "very often" when watching television.[12] The good news (at least for advertisers) is that they're using their other screens to stay engaged with what they're watching, with 71% reporting that they switched screens to look up something about what they were watching, to email or message someone about what's on the screen (41%), to look up or shop for a product being advertised (35%), or to post something to social media (28%).

Nevertheless, in the multi-screen, simultaneous-viewing world, television isn't faring well. In a laboratory study conducted by YuMe, a multi-screen video advertising technology company, it turned out that, while test subjects favored TV the most as compared to other devices (53% of the time), they also spent less than half the time paying attention to it when other devices were available. In fact, the YuMe study found that the attention span while watching television dropped from the initial rate of 53% to a dismal 19% after only four minutes of simultaneous viewing. And this trend could get worse. A study on TV watching habits conducted by Millward Brown found that 36% of respondents admitted that they weren't really watching TV at all. It was "just background noise."

Why is this a big deal? Simply put, if these numbers are generalized to the entire TV watching population (or, at the very least, the 81% who own smartphones[13]), it means that a big chunk of the TV audience doesn't "consume" it. Chances are good that the TV is on but, attention-wise, nobody's home.

So, what's a marketer to do in the multi-screen world of today? For many, the answer is to throw up as much ad content as possible across as many screens as possible in hopes that it will stick. While wildly buying ad space is never a good idea, there is something to be said about considering all possible screens.

As consulting giant PwC says in their Global Entertainment and Media Outlook report: "Internet advertising will increasingly become device agnostic … advertisers should be asking what types of content generate greatest consumer engagement rather than whether people are reading a website on a mobile device or not."[14] It's a sentiment they echo in their 2019 version of the report.[15] Looking at the media landscape as a whole, PwC observes: "The central theme of this world of growing media is that it's personal and increasingly digital."

In short, the era of mass media is over. People now consume media when they want, where they want, and on whichever device they prefer.

The Funnel Becomes a Loop

With all the ways that changes in technology have changed people's habits, are the time-honored understandings of how audiences make decisions out-of-date? We think so. And we think we know what's changing.

But first, let's look at the way we traditionally think about audience decision-making: the funnel. In this interpretation of the sales process, a prospect moves from interest to purchase, following a series of discrete steps along the way. In higher education, the belief in the funnel results in a familiar pattern every recruitment season: Lock down your creative, build out your landing pages, tweak your forms, buy your lists and ads, send out mailings and emails, then sit back and wait.

Not all of your targets will click an ad or submit an RFI, but for the ones that do, BAM! They're in the funnel. Then it's time to work that flow with some emails and they're as good as yours.

But if it's that easy, why are so many schools hurting for enrollment?

While there are a myriad of reasons enrollments are down, it's hard not to attribute a portion of the problem to the fact that our sales process hasn't changed despite the major changes in the ways audiences behave. Sure, the funnel may apply when you buy something impulsively; that's why grocery stores put those irresistible treats on the endcaps near the checkout counter. They're assuming you won't do any research or gather opinions from your friends on social media before you toss those ChocoMarshy SaltySnax in your cart. But such assumptions fall apart for anything that isn't an impulse buy.

Thanks to the huge amount of available information and the transition of mass media into increasingly personal media, consumers' decision-making journeys are a lot less direct than they were in the past, particularly for anything that's considered a "big" purchase. In the Digital Age, the funnel has stopped being a funnel. It's become a loop.

That isn't to say there's *no* linear progression — attention-interest-action still defines the basic decision-making process — but modern audiences take a much more winding path. Because of this, you should get used to spreading your marketing efforts along the entire student lifecycle, rather than clustering all your resources near the top of the proverbial funnel. And you should understand a few important new facts:

1. Timing promotions has limited value. This is especially true in higher ed as the population of prospects moves further away from the traditional high school teenager with a singular focus on college to a more complex population of teens and adults at various stages of their life experience.

2. Media matters. People use different media for different reasons. An ad forwarded by (or endorsed by) a friend has a different impact on a consumer than an ad that pops up unbidden online. A text message is more personal than a banner. You get the idea.

3. Customers can be powerful advocates. One post to a timeline or one tweet can potentially voice pleasure (or displeasure) to hundreds or even thousands of others. Thinking that the sales funnel ends after a purchase is nuts. In many ways, it's just beginning.

4. Attention isn't what it used to be. If people didn't care much about your messages in the Analog Age, they care infinitely less today.

5. The consumer is now in control. The digital age shifted power from producer to consumer and from hierarchies to networks. Therefore, the sales process is much less about guiding consumers to a purchase decision and a lot more about giving them the information and tools they need to move themselves to a purchase decision. This is a critical distinction. Marketers, give it up. You're no longer in control.

So how do these new realities impact higher ed marketers? To answer that as clearly as possible, we'll look at an example of a specific audience. One who:

- Decides to enroll in a professional graduate program.
- Completes the program.
- Has the potential to become a life-long advocate or brand ambassador for the school.

First, let's look at how the traditional recruitment sales funnel would treat our audience.

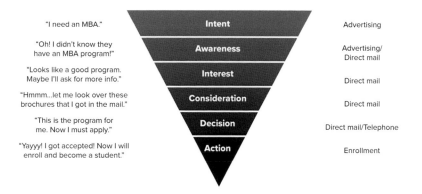

PROSPECT		CONTACT MEDIUM
"I need an MBA."	**Intent**	Advertising
"Oh! I didn't know they have an MBA program!"	**Awareness**	Advertising/ Direct mail
"Looks like a good program. Maybe I'll ask for more info."	**Interest**	Direct mail
"Hmmm...let me look over these brochures that I got in the mail."	**Consideration**	Direct mail
"This is the program for me. Now I must apply."	**Decision**	Direct mail/Telephone
"Yayyy! I got accepted! Now I will enroll and become a student."	**Action**	Enrollment

We're sure that looks familiar to you. But, as we've discussed, most of the assumptions presented in the graphic don't represent new realities. The audience won't only be coming to you. They're going to do some intensive online research, look at numerous school websites, reach out to their social networks, and maybe even ask questions on forums. And, as they're going through this process, they may be asking questions that are a lot broader than, "Where do I get my MBA?" They may be asking, "Do I even need an MBA?" "Would a different degree be better?" "Should I forget grad school altogether?"

On top of that, we need to consider what happens if they do enroll with us. Are they going to stay? Are they going to tell others about their experience? Even if they go somewhere else, it's still a good bet that they're going to tell others about their experience with us, affecting someone else's decisions down the line.

The funnel fails to capture the ways modern audiences make decisions at the beginning of the sales process and the ways their actions continue to impact the sales process even after we've stopped interacting with them.

So, let's look at a better way
of thinking about the process:

1 **CONSIDER SCHOOL**
Generate an interest:
Webinars, Blogs, Social content.

2 **DISCOVER OPTIONS**
Position your school as a contender:
Personalized website, Email, Social,
Chat, Webinars, Open houses.

3 **LIST CONSIDERED SCHOOLS**
Differentiate your school:
Personalized website, Email,
Social, Chat, Webinars, Open houses,
Calls from alumni or faculty,
Long form content.

4 **WEIGH TOP OPTIONS**
Facilitate "best fit":
Personalized website, Periodic reminder emails,
Social, Telephone support, Long form content.

5 **APPLY**
Encourage applications:
Personalized website,
Administrative support,
Financial aid.

6 **ENROLL**
Reafirm student's desicion:
Email, Social media, Events,
Telephone support.

7 **FIRST YEAR
EXPERIENCE**
Encourage retention:
Student life community,
Academic support,
Facilitated advocacy,
Social media.

8 **CONNECTIONS
& COMMUNITY**
Create a bond:
Department/program events,
Personal contact,
Career preperation.

9 **LAST YEAR EXPERIENCE**
Support student's next steps:
Events, Alumni connection,
Career center support.

10 **ALUMNI & ADVANCEMENT**
Encourage involvement and advocacy:
Continued career support, Alumni events,
Continuing education, Encourage referrals.

**Full Circle
Marketing**

KEY
STAGE OF STUDENT JOURNEY
Goal of University
Tactics for Reaching University Goal

In the loop model, the recruitment process operates on an entirely new set of principles that takes into account seven modern realities.

1. You can't predict when someone's going to want to pursue a professional graduate education.

2. People have questions that arise at each stage that need to be answered.

3. To answer their questions, people turn to different forms of media — and you have to be nimble and responsive enough to meet their needs wherever they are.

4. Making a decision doesn't happen in a vacuum.

5. Decisions are made with verbs, not nouns. It's an active process, not a series of discrete stages.

6. Once the decision has been made, customers can become advocates — or ex-customers.

7. The sales process never ends. And, if it does, you're doing something wrong.

Applying these new principles doesn't mean throwing out everything you know. Instead, it means thinking about your prospects as participants rather than as passive recipients of your messages. And it means recognizing that no sale is final. You're looking to develop lifelong customers and advocates.

Let's explore this in terms of our example audience, beginning with prospects who aren't even sold on the idea of going to graduate school. To reach a prospect at this stage (#1 on The Full Circle Marketing diagram), you have to cast a wide net. Social media, public relations/earned media, and content marketing are good places to start. Focus on creating content that's useful to those who might be thinking about the next stage of their career and promote the concept that going to grad school is a good option for professional growth. This content doesn't even need to be branded. After all, you don't want them to perceive your content as advertising. You're just trying to get some portion of your prospects to think, "Hey! Maybe I need to go to graduate school."

And what do you do when they're ready to explore their options (#2 on The Full Circle Marketing diagram)? First, don't assume they have the same kind of knowledge about professional graduate programs that you do. That's a quick way to lose them. Instead, think of these prospects as explorers entering unknown territory. And the best way to reach explorers is through the main path of modern exploration: search engines.

Creating online destinations designed for prospects exploring professional graduate schools gives these prospects something useful to find during their search engine exploration, assuming you've done good SEO (more on that in our chapter on traffic). These destinations should focus on the information that prospects want and not hit them over the head to take an action. They're not ready for that. However, these destinations should be branded content and it's great if they give details (cost, time-to-completion, etc.) for a specific program or set of programs.

At this point, some prospects may take a step back and reconsider the value of graduate education. That's OK. For those who do engage with you (#3-4 on The Full Circle Marketing diagram), you'll finally have the opportunity to use a lot of your traditional marketing techniques. But you'll want to work in some new ones too. Again, you can't assume that someone is engaging with you because you moved them there. They may have taken a much more circuitous path — they may not even be sure they want to go to graduate school yet — so their presence at this stage is often tenuous at best.

Your job is to help reinforce their desire to go to the next phase in their careers/lives and make that as easy as possible. To help them choose to take the next step with you, get closer to them. Nurture the relationship with personalized websites tailored to their interests, helpful emails reminding them of important dates, and long-form content about what to expect (especially if they've been out of school for a while). In addition, be available, both online and on the phone, so you can answer questions when prospects ask them. If done right, you'll overcome all the obstacles between someone who is engaged and someone who becomes an applicant.

But once they have applied (#5 on The Full Circle Marketing diagram), your job isn't done. Even if prospects don't apply anywhere else, they still might decide to walk away from the decision. Your goal at this stage is to get them to enroll (#6 on The Full Circle Marketing diagram), keeping up that personal contact through the web, email, social media, or over the phone.

It's an investment of time and resources that will pay big dividends later. As all higher ed marketers know, melt is a big problem, one made even bigger with the advent of the Common App and the ease of applying online. But if you've built relationships with your prospects as early as possible, been responsive, and assisted them with the process of applying, you'll have a much better chance of keeping them after their acceptance.

However, as you've likely guessed, just because your prospects have accepted and become students, your job is still not through. Except now, it's all about providing a good customer experience (#7-9 on The Full Circle Marketing diagram). We know the term "customer experience" can make many in the academic world head for the hills, but, like it or not, students *are* your customers and they have good or bad customer experiences. You can help these experiences be good by staying in touch with students and letting them know that you care. Occasional emails asking how things are going or offering advising help if they have run into a snag can have a big impact.

This kind of personalized attention should continue even after students graduate. In the loop, everyone who intersects with your brand can influence other people's perceptions and decision-making process. And former students make the best brand champions (#10 on The Full Circle Marketing diagram), reinforcing the cycle and helping generate future students. The more you interact with them, the more likely they are to become your advocates.

In the current environment, you can't simply sift prospects through a tired linear progression to a single and absolute end. You have to think much more holistically, creating the information and experiences your audiences want at whatever stage they're at. The more you meet their needs and expectations at every stage, the more you can use the modern decision-making process to your advantage.

Forget the funnel. Embrace the loop.

Connecting with Your Audience Segments

It's one thing to know about modern audiences and their decision-making process, but if you're going to truly connect to your audience segments, you need to see them not as numbers or abstract concepts, but as human beings with thoughts, feelings, motivations, and free will. In order to achieve this and to gain empathy for the people we're communicating with, designers, usability experts, and developers create what are known as personas and use them to test ideas, approaches, designs, products, and services.

Personas aren't real people. Instead, they're stand-ins, representing how we think real people might act based on how we define them. They are not meant to be stereotypes, but rather, archetypes. While personas aren't "real," their situations, motivations, and actions are quite real, at least in the aggregate.

In higher education, you can use personas to map the wants and needs of real audiences to your institution's offerings. For example, if you offer an undergraduate program and three graduate programs, you could create four personas to represent the people who are interested in those programs, as long as the needs and behaviors of your audiences for those programs are distinct enough to warrant the separate personas. As you dive into the project, however, you may find that you'll need to create additional personas to capture the finer distinctions between the audiences you're trying to represent.

Creating Personas

To create a persona of a prospective student, you'll want to do some research with your target audiences. The following questions can serve as a good starting place, but you may have other, more specific questions you want to ask. No matter how you go, remember that the personas you create need to be based on reality, not your own perceptions of how you think your audiences might think, feel, and behave.

- Why do you want to earn this degree?
- How do you think this degree will impact your life?
- Who, if anyone, will help you make this decision?
- What are your apprehensions?
- How does who you are (age, gender, income, etc.) impact your decision?
- How does your physical location affect your decision?
- What is your timeline to make a decision?

Personas don't have to be complicated or time-consuming to create. If they ring true as reasonable facsimiles of the people you're trying to communicate with, they will work. To help make them seem more "real" for your team, give each persona a name and use stock photography to represent their physical presence. The better you define each audience, the more meaningful your marketing decisions can be.

As an example of how this process works, let's say that you've been tasked with promoting your institution's online MBA program. You're at a public institution, so you don't have a huge budget and must spend your media money wisely. In this situation, personas can be quite useful. To create them, all you have to do is look at your audience segments.

In our scenario, one of several audience segments you've identified is "Ambitious Working Moms." It's a segment defined by being female, married with kids, and heading toward the early-middle part of a career. "Ambitious Working Moms" deferred graduate studies to have children, but they are career-driven and eager to overcome the time/work experience they lost by staying at home when their children were infants. While they still have childcare responsibilities, their kids are reaching school age and they've recently returned to the workforce, so they've begun to think about earning a graduate degree as a way of accelerating their careers.

That insight might be enough to start developing creative and laying out a media plan, but it becomes a lot easier if you develop a more well-rounded and personalized picture of "Ambitious Working Moms" through a persona. Your research into this segment has also revealed that members of this segment tend to be avid consumers of news, frequently participate in social media, and tend to be more on the moderate to conservative end of the political spectrum. In your area, they tend to cluster in the inner suburbs or in the more affluent parts of the city where the public schools are better. Through those insights, you can develop a persona.

While obviously not every member of the segment is going to be the same, giving "Patricia Prospect" a full life can help focus your thinking.

EXAMPLE PERSONA

DEMOGRAPHICS

32 Years Old
Female
San Francisco, CA

Married, 2 Children
(ages 3 and 5)

Accountant

BS, Business
HHI: $130,000/year

Patricia Prospect
Ambitious Working Mom

 It's been a while since I've been in the classroom. I can't wait to meet other students just like me.

I AM MOTIVATED BY...
Price and online/hybrid learning styles. I'm also looking to start soon, hopefully within the next 3-6 months.

I AM LOOKING TO...
Earn an MBA or MS in Finance to jump start my career and grow professionally.

I AM CONCERNED ABOUT...
Overall cost of tuition and flexible learning methods. Balancing my family life with my graduate school program is very important to me.

MY DAY-TO-DAY LOOKS LIKE...
Wake up. Kids. Commute. Work. Commute. Kids. Dinner. Bath. Tuck-in. Browse the internet on my phone. Sleep.

YOU CAN REACH ME BY...
Social media, my local newspaper (online), cable news, local talk radio.

OTHER THINGS IMPORTANT TO ME ARE...
Earning a degree from a reputable program that will help me get a job right after graduation.

Rather than just being a set of demographics and statistics, Patricia Prospect becomes a real person to whom you and your team can ascribe motivations and behaviors based on what you know about her. And since you know her better through her persona, you can start developing creative that's going to resonate with her.

Please note that the sample we're including here is just an example. If you have more data about your audiences, feel free to develop your own persona format that includes it. If you have less, go with less. Come up with your own formats. Improvise. The important thing is that your personas help your team gain empathy for your audience segments. They're people, not numbers.

Think about Patricia as described by the persona. She's busy and spends a fair amount of time commuting to work. Considering how young her kids are, it's going to be a while before she can devote a lot of time to school, so she's most likely looking for a part-time, online program that gives her the flexibility to be in control of her progress. While she enjoys a comfortable lifestyle, she's not rich by any stretch, making cost a big concern. She's well-informed, so she's probably going to want as much detail about your program as you can give her. She's ambitious but a little nervous about how going back to school is going to impact her life, so she's going to want to know that whatever institution she chooses will provide the support and resources she needs, 24/7 if possible. She's still weighing the costs and benefits of an MBA or an MS in Finance, so she's going to be searching for both when researching what school to go to. Her choices locally are somewhat limited. It's either your institution or the small, private nonprofit institution that offers similar graduate business degrees.

Nationally, of course, she could look at the big for-profit online schools. While you might be worried that you'll struggle to compete with those big for-profits, if you consider the whole persona, you'll worry less. Patricia is concerned with both support and with the reputation of the institution she gets her degree from (remember, she's a professional in a competitive industry who's already making up for lost time). While she might be able to get the flexibility she wants at a cost that makes sense for her at a for-profit school, it's likely that she's going to go local with her choice.

So, is that local private nonprofit institution going to be competition? Probably, but considering the premium they charge for tuition, they'll be more difficult for Patricia to afford than your institution will be. Yes, they have a higher reputation among local employers, but someone like Patricia may take the more prudent, pragmatic approach and go with your school, provided she knows about your programs and knows what you're about.

With these insights, you can begin to imagine creative that's going to appeal to people like Patricia — creative that emphasizes your supportive approach to graduate business education, your program's flexibility, and the value of the degree. Because Patricia may be nervous about taking the leap, you may want to use encouraging, future-forward copy and imagery that allows her to see herself as a successful student who has what it takes to earn her degree.

In order to reach her, focus on the media she consumes. The online version of the local paper might be a bargain, especially if they have packages available that combine print and online editions. She commutes to work, so out-of-home might be an economical option too. And, because you are local and have a downtown campus near the business district, holding informational open houses can allow Patricia to experience your faculty and staff face-to-face, offering a personal touch that a big online university can't provide. If you follow the insights the persona offers, it probably won't be long before Patricia Prospect is a student.

Yes, personas are generalizations, but they're useful generalizations based on research that can focus thinking, spur creative thought, and help you see the connections between otherwise dry and siloed data you've collected about your prospects. It's hard to get inspired by raw numbers, but when you can get to know who you're marketing to through the use of personas, you'll be inspired to take your marketing to a whole new level.

THE CREATIVE
PROCESS

89

When you've completed your research, refined your strategy, and identified precisely who you're speaking to, it's time to focus on tactics. As discussed, we separate the tactics of a successful marketing plan into three distinct pillars: traffic, destination, and nurture. But before we dive into those tactics, we need to talk about the one core element they share: creativity.

Creativity is what it takes to create something new. And new is exactly what you want your marketing campaign to be. If it looks and sounds like everything you've done before — or like everything others have done before — then your campaign won't make much of an impact.

However, in the world of marketing, being new isn't enough, which is why, when we talk about creativity, we're talking about more than pure inventiveness. We're talking about the act of creating something that has a purpose and successfully fulfills that purpose. In the case of higher education (and in most other industries), the purpose of marketing is to attract attention and spur action. That's your goal. And the pursuit of that goal is called the creative process.

Even if you hire a creative firm to handle the creative aspects of your marketing campaign, you'll still be involved in the creative process.

You'll help establish the strategy and you'll give the final approval or disapproval. That's a lot of responsibility. If you're handling the creative aspects yourself, that's even more responsibility. To make the best decisions, you need an understanding of how certain creative elements work and why they matter. This chapter is here to help you gain that understanding.

Why Design Matters (More than Ever)

In a time of intense competition and the ever-increasing noise of commercial messages, getting noticed is less about what you spend and more about creating compelling content that engages your target audiences. Quality, not quantity, is the key.

In other words, design matters.

Design is about more than how something looks. It's also about how it functions in the world. A gorgeous dress would still be considered poorly designed if it doesn't fit the human form or if no one can wear it without tripping on the hem. Likewise, your mailer may have striking photography and hand-lettered labels, but if it's difficult to unfold or too expensive to mail, it's a design failure

The best design does multiple things well.

1. It's pleasing to experience.
2. It communicates what it's meant for.
3. It's simple to use.

While the first of those is often a matter of taste — and tastes change over time — the other two are far more universal. Ancient Roman roads were so well designed that people still travel on some of them today. Shakespeare's plays were so well designed (writing is linguistic design) that they're still performed all over the world.

So, what makes the best design these days? Technology has always influenced design and, in a world saturated by technology, this link is stronger than ever. Specifically, it's spurred a cultural preference for designs with usability. This focus on the third element of good design has resulted in a push toward a reduction in adornment, an emphasis on usefulness, and a natural pairing of form with function.

These days, poor brand usability at any touchpoint is not only seen as a design faux pas, it's seen as intolerable. We want our products and services to be easy to obtain, easy to use, easy to integrate into our lives, and super easy to fix if needed. It's a truth worth remembering, whether you're producing traffic-generating content (it better be easy to respond to), destination content (it better be easy to understand), or nurture content (it better fit easily into a prospect's life).

We've seen the shift to usability with many recent consumer-facing product battles. The original Apple iPhone launch stands out as the megaphone (pun intended) that told the world that a highly technical and complex device didn't have to be confusing or ugly. Instead, it could feel natural. Then there's the example of Facebook dethroning MySpace (remember them?) by offering a clean, minimal interface that was hyper-focused on only a few utilitarian features. Since then, Apple, Facebook, Google, Amazon, and others have defined the barrier to entry for digital brand experiences through their standardized, atomic user interfaces (UI).

Yes, it's true that part of this desire for ultra-usability is due to a shift in cultural preferences. But even if we shift back toward more ornamentalism in design, it's essential to realize that, regardless of the tastes of the moment, excellent design is the foundation to successful marketing. Higher education, in particular, already faces an uphill battle in getting the eyes of prospects and donors. If you squander the opportunity to build your brand because your points of connection are poorly designed, you're wasting your marketing dollars.

Great design requires thinking about much more than "Do I like the logo?" or "Do I like the color pallete?" Those choices matter, but what matters more is the totality of your campaign's design. All of the pieces you design — from the photography in a mailer to the functionality of a website to the words in an email — need to fit together in a way that feels good, makes sense, and successfully moves your target market from prospect to enrolled student, and then ultimately to engaged alumnus.

The Future of Design: Brand Experience

One of the difficulties every brand faces is the fact that design styles change. And not just because tastes change. Advancements in technology will often remake what's possible, and that will, in turn, change our expectations of how things should be designed. Before the internet, we printed marketing materials. Now, we expect every organization to have a website. And if they don't have a website, we're likely to question more than their design choices. We may question their credibility as a business.

But just having a website isn't enough either. It needs to be a modern website. Before the smartphone arrived, designers conceptualized most websites in the same way they thought about annual reports. The content was organized logically, often in a linear sequence. Screen layouts were optimized to make it easier to read long-form content. More content required? Just repeat the same formula.

New screen sizes demanded new rules. Responsive design (websites that resize themselves to match the size of the viewing screen) was a critical step in making sure that various devices could access valuable content. Now, if a website doesn't use responsive design and thus functions poorly on our smartphones, we question the credibility — or at least the modernity — of the organization almost as much as we would question them if they had no website at all.

Clearly, your design has to keep up with the technology and the resulting expectations of the audience. What does that mean for the near future? It likely means designing for devices and apps whose interactions don't always, or ever, happen on a screen.

As we continue to enter the Internet of Things era — where fitness bands track vital signs, buttons on washing machines order more detergent, and social apps communicate to us on the go — we need to start thinking beyond the look of webpages and consider how we can express an institution's brand in any medium and on any device, even if that device has no screen. That's the future. And, in many respects, the future is already here.

For example, there's a good chance you've used a screenless device within the last 24 hours. According to PwC's *Consumer Intelligence* series, 59% of 18- to 24-year-olds, 65% of 25- to 49-year-olds, and 57% of people over 50 report using their voices to interact with their digital devices at least once a day.[16] Out of the consumers surveyed, 71% reported that they would rather use their voices to search for information than have to type their searches the traditional way.

Considering the proliferation of anti-handheld phone driving laws, the explosion of smart speakers, such as Amazon's Alexa (100 million sold as of the beginning of 2019[17]), and the vast improvements in the reliability of AI products, such as Apple's Siri and Google Assistant, it's not surprising that more of us are turning to voice as our preferred choice when it comes to interacting with our devices. But the shift from visual to vocal interaction will require a shift in how we think about branding.

For most brands, that will mean thinking about design as not just visuals and words but as a holistic brand experience, identifiable anywhere it's encountered. What will this look like? Disney provides some clues.

What began as an animation studio is now a beloved brand with a brand experience we recognize the moment we encounter it. The company has achieved this level of branding by continually rethinking what design can be and how far it can reach. Their branding is not just the classic silhouette of Mickey Mouse or the tagline, "The Happiest Place on Earth." It stretches much further and includes the hopeful first notes of "When You Wish Upon a Star," the comforting smell of cinnamon rolls as you walk down their theme park's Main Street U.S.A., and the joyful ease with which its many websites function. And, recently, it includes the MagicBands that allow guests at Disney parks to access rides, buy food and souvenirs, meet characters, and generally glide through the park as if by, well, magic. And magic is exactly what the Disney brand experience is designed to be about.

While not every organization has the resources of Disney, every organization should be looking at how Disney treats design. Because the future of design is a future of brand experiences. As designers and innovators, we must think beyond the look and interface of what we're designing and reflect on what an organization's brand experience is at its core and how that translates to the marketing we're creating next.

In higher education, designing a brand experience that attracts donors, students, faculty, partners, and others will require thinking beyond websites and landing pages. We will still use them as conversion touchpoints, but websites and landing pages should be the bridges that lead to other brand experiences, including campus open houses, campus signage, call scripts, workflow design (e.g., designing the follow-up schedules with leads), and every other element that serves as a connection point between you and your audience. In short, the higher education brand needs to become ever-present and accessible at the precise moment a prospect needs it, creating a brand experience that's as consistent as it is powerful.

Creating a Brand Experience

Given what we know about the future of design, we can safely say that the creative process needs to be about more than creating logos, headlines, websites, and emails. It needs to be about integrating all of that and more to create a brand experience. But how do you go about doing that?

The first step is recognizing *what* you're doing. Brand experiences are, at their heart, about building a deep, emotional bond that feels natural and personal. Experiencing your brand should create attachment and engagement, not just familiarity. Familiarity is easy; it just takes repetition. Emotional connections take more. Here are a few steps you can take to connect emotionally and create a successful and unique brand experience.

Think beyond the "graphic." Across print, broadcast, and digital, recognize that your brand experience as everything in-between. Rethink tangible touchpoints and design collateral to support and extend larger brand and marketing efforts. Consider how a brand experience can be crafted through in-person exchanges, personalized environmental interactions such as on-campus displays, and non-disposable take-homes utilizing the capabilities of apps and devices.

Conduct field research. Run usability tests on today's applications to identify market and brand opportunities for improvement. Conduct prospect interviews, focus groups, and collaborative sketching studios with prospects and stakeholders, rather than following the higher education herd.

Understand, map, and redesign workflows. Use test findings to map out and understand internal and external workflows, journeys, and processes. Evaluate the day-to-day pressures and decisions of recruiters to build campaign and tracking tools that aid in relationship building. Fully understand the prospect decision-making journey and life cycle in order to improve existing touch points and minimize the possibility of prospects falling through the cracks.

Establish and extend atomic brand libraries. Build cohesive brand UI libraries across digital applications and printed collateral — iconography, photography style, code components and widgets, grid systems and templates, and even brand language. A useful brand library is much more than fonts and colors. Build the library as a flexible brand foundation, not as a rigid and over-policed system. That will make it easier for growth and refinement.

Identify and update key touch points. Review what you know about the workflows and journeys to identify low-hanging fruit and particularly problematic engagement points. Use that knowledge to develop new brand assets, new experiences, and better conversion tools, one at a time. Avoid overhauling everything at once, which often increases the chance of failure.

Designers are the fuel for each of these efforts. Fill out your team with a blend of visual designers, researchers and statisticians, interactive designers, copywriters, and interface developers. A multi-disciplinary blend is integral to innovating in the higher education space and it can keep you focused on designing brand experiences and not just designing the next mailer or website.

Tomorrow's successful higher education brands will divert marketing budgets to brand experience designers who can build emotional connections that lead to lasting relationships. For these institutions, design will take center stage. And their brand experience will be the most valuable property they own.

Avoiding Design Battleship

Before any piece of marketing — let alone an entire brand experience plan — enters the world, it must be approved by stakeholders within your organization. Maybe that means getting the sign-off from the university president, or perhaps it means getting the sign-off from a committee of a dozen or more individuals. But regardless of the approval process at your institution, there's one problem you should work hard to avoid; a problem we call "design battleship."

If you've presented design previously, you'll recognize the all-too-common pattern of pitch, change, pitch again, change again, pitch yet again, and so on, until it feels like no decision will ever be made. In these situations, no one is happy and little gets done.

That is design battleship. Just like the board game where players take turns calling out different coordinates to try to hit the opposing player's ships, design battleship can be maddening because you're aiming for a target you can't see. Except, in the game, the board is a 10-by-10 grid and, eventually, you'll hit something. In design battleship, the grid feels infinite and hitting anything seems impossible.

While there are a lot of causes for design battleship, we've found that the main culprit is subjective criteria. Anything that's open to an opinion has the potential to be misinterpreted and misunderstood. If you're lucky, everyone's individual tastes eventually align and a design is chosen. If not, things can go south quickly.

To avoid design battleship, it's important for everyone involved to develop and agree to a set of objective criteria for judging what's presented. That way, you can eliminate — or at least reduce — subjectivity.

For example, if the designers and approval committee all agree to evaluate a design based on how well it aligns with the overall strategy of the project, the feedback received through target audience focus groups, and the functional requirements of the project, the fact that one person doesn't like the color yellow won't send the entire endeavor back to the drawing board. Because a color choice can be evaluated by the previously agreed-upon criteria. It doesn't have to be left to the whims of one person's tastes.

As we like to say, "Every pixel (and ink dot) should have a purpose." When everyone agrees on that purpose before anything is even designed, you can avoid the Sisyphean misery of design battleship. And that will make designing everything that the three pillars require much more successful.

Case Study: The Power of Brand Experience

Love 'em or hate 'em, *U.S. News & World Report's* rankings really do influence prospective student choice. And while most institutions struggle to move up the rankings, our client had a particularly difficult problem: how to stay in the top five.

The answer might seem simple: Keep doing what you're doing. But the reality is a lot more complex. Rankings aren't just determined by objective criteria, such as starting salaries of graduates or how long it takes them to get jobs. They're also determined by a number of subjective rankings, not the least of which is rankings from leaders of peer institutions.

We knew that we couldn't affect graduation rates or alumni success, but we believed we *could* have an impact on how the institution was perceived by its peers. In other words, if we could augment the brand experience in a way that elevated peer perceptions, we could help our client retain their ranking.

But the answer couldn't be redesigning the website. The current site was huge and we didn't have the time to change it in order to impact the overall brand experience. The answer had to come from elsewhere and, after much deliberation and collaboration with our client, we landed on it: Celebrate the accomplishments of the previous year.

The school was doing great work, conducting research and developing innovations that made millions of people's lives better. These discoveries and inventions weren't always front-page news, but they were the kinds of discoveries that peers in the field would understand and appreciate. They just had to know about them.

To better promote the university's accomplishments and enhance the brand experience for its peers, we designed a website dedicated to chronicling the major achievements of the previous year, delivered in a way that reinforced the overall brand and positioned the university as *the* leader in its field.

We went to work on two fronts. Our designers worked tirelessly to develop a way of presenting the stories so that each felt fresh and yet part of a larger, unified story. Our copywriters went to work mining the school's publications (both academic and otherwise) to uncover the biggest discoveries of the year. When we found them, we wrote them up in a way that would appeal to the scientific community — a big part of the audience — as well as to an informed public of professionals in non-research roles who were also in the field. Then we combined the innovative design and content into a new website that told a cohesive story encapsulating the school's previous year.

Designing with brand experience in mind must have worked. The university is still holding the top position they've occupied for decades.

—

The future of design is a future of brand experiences.

THE FIRST PILLAR: TRAFFIC

103

The most visible (and measurable) part of any marketing campaign is the traffic that it generates. It's exciting to do something out in the world and then see the effort bear fruit in the form of people coming to your website, leads pouring into your admissions office, or people showing up at an open house. These are the kinds of things that set marketers' hearts aflutter. They're measurable, real, and you can report them to your boss.

But, traffic is costly and will almost certainly be the area where you make the largest investment. Whether you're spending big (e.g., TV advertising) or small (e.g., paid search), everything will require an expenditure. That might tempt you to hedge your bets and spread your money around equally to try as many options as you can afford.

Don't.

The far better strategy is to use integrated marketing. Instead of throwing money at everything (or just one thing), you should carefully choose which media to use so as to create synergy between them, creating something bigger than the sum of its parts.

For example, if you're running an out-of-home media campaign, also consider (if you can swing it financially) releasing online banners and paid social media posts with the same creative/message and call to action. The traditional media push will lower the digital campaign's click barrier by increasing familiarity with your brand among target audiences. Digital outreach will similarly enhance the effectiveness of traditional media and add value to each rollout.

Flexibility is another key to effective traffic-generating campaigns. No plan is bulletproof. Some aspects may penetrate more quickly or effectively than others. Designing your strategy to incorporate flexibility will be crucial to your ability to respond in real-time to the ongoing results of your efforts.

Traditional media still offers the greatest opportunity to disseminate your message broadly. Unfortunately, most traditional media outlets, such as TV, radio, out-of-home (with the exception of digital billboards), and transit, don't allow for much — if any — flexibility to change creative content during a campaign's run. If your traffic-generating plan includes traditional media (and most likely it will), make sure you think through each media outlet's restrictions, including limitations to cancellations or mid-run changes to the media flight. In cases where the medium presents barriers to creative flexibility, focus that portion of your integrated marketing on brand awareness and basic messaging. These are less likely to change once the campaign is in full swing.

Digital media, on the other hand, can combine the flexibility you need with a more targeted version of the mass-communication qualities of traditional media. Digital radio, digital billboards, and streaming video pre-rolls, to name a few options, allow for hyper-specific audience segmentation, and also let you increase, decrease, suspend, or shift your spending based on performance. You may not always be able to use digital media, but when you do, your campaign will benefit from its capacity to support both branding and directly actionable audience engagement. In other words, digital allows you to augment the branding power and reach of traditional media with greater flexibility, targeting, and real-time performance optimization.

Always keep timing and flexibility in mind when engineering traffic-generating media campaigns. If possible, design campaigns for dual duties: to build awareness via traditional mass marketing and to swap digital creative in and out at a moment's notice.

Traffic in the Digital Age

The concept of traffic can be elusive in the Digital Age. Attention and engagement are challenging to measure, and raw numbers alone aren't always a reliable indicator of whether your traffic-generating efforts are working, since taking action online requires minimal effort.

In this section, we'll dig into some of the difficulties you might face when trying to generate traffic. Then, we'll offer suggestions for dealing with the ephemeral nature of traffic in the digital world by looking at today's multi-screen reality, search marketing, search engine optimization (SEO), social media, and content marketing.

The Four Dimensions of the Multi-Screen Universe

As we previously discussed, there are *many* ways for people to consume information and entertainment. To understand how this relatively new reality affects the way we can and should drive traffic, we need to understand the dimensions of multi-screen use.

Dimension 1: Audience

We have to know with whom we're trying to communicate. From the research on screen usage, it's pretty clear that factors such as age, socioeconomic status, gender, and ethnicity influence the types of screens people use and when. For younger, non-white people with low incomes and low levels of educational attainment, their portal to the digital world is most likely smartphones, according to Pew.[18] More affluent people are likely to have more screens available. However, usage seems to correspond mostly to age, which also affects our second dimension.

Dimension 2: Intention

The reason someone is using a particular device has a significant impact on where they are in the multi-screen universe. If they're doing in-depth research on products or services, creating content other than photographs or video, or working, they're likely using a desktop or laptop computer. These devices, with multiple inputs, large screens, and ample storage, lend themselves to such activities. On the other hand, if they're commenting on a movie they're watching, entertaining themselves while waiting in line, trying to navigate their physical space, checking prices on goods or services, or documenting their travels, they're likely using a smartphone or tablet.

Dimension 3: Context

Context, (where someone is or their circumstances) also influences what people do and which screen they choose. Teenagers stuck watching the news with Grandma will be on their phone as soon as they can sneak it out. If someone's at work, they'll be on a desktop or laptop.

Dimension 4: Device

The characteristics of a particular device influences user behavior. Smartphones, with their portability, always-on data connection, and a trove of preferences, become very personal. That translates to frequent usage over the course of a day, serving as a connector, boredom-killer, on-the-spot advisor, and navigator.

On the other hand, laptop and desktop computers function as tools of creation, portals to information, number crunchers, and organizers of all the information we collect throughout our lives. Tablets are somewhere in between, performing many of the functions reserved for laptops and desktops in a personal way. Meanwhile, smartwatches are mostly tied to our smartphones and give us an additional way to access our mobile devices.

Targeting in the Multi-Screen Universe

Once we understand the properties of the four dimensions, we can develop marketing communications that work best.

For example, let's say you want to reach 16- to 18-year-olds who are searching for colleges. Since you know your audience and their intention, you can infer context (probably at home) and device (laptop or desktop computer). Why? Because they need to research large amounts of information and organize it for future reference. You can assume that they're at home because research shows us that, if they're out and about, they're using their smartphones to access the internet for something other than looking for a college.

- **AUDIENCE:** Prospective students between the ages of 16 and 18 who are interested in attending college.
- **INTENTION:** They want to pick a college that's right for them.
- **CONTEXT:** In their homes focused on searching.
- **DEVICE:** Laptop or desktop, either in a bedroom or a communal area in the home.

So, what do you do with this information? First, use what you know about your audience to craft a message. Next, since the audience is engaged in a search, consider paid search or listings on college ranking websites. At home, prospective students have time to read more information than if they were on their phones, meaning you have the opportunity to engage them with longer messages. Thanks to the processing speed of laptops and desktops, you can even utilize high-definition videos and/or graphically intense interactive experiences, like virtual tours.

However, let's say that the same prospective students have chosen a set of schools to visit and they're on their way to campus for the first time. You can safely assume that they're in the process of traveling and using a smartphone, so you can adjust your dimensions accordingly:

- **AUDIENCE**: Prospective students between the ages of 16 and 18 who have developed a shortlist of schools to visit.
- **INTENTION**: They want to pick a college that's right for them.
- **CONTEXT**: Traveling to campus for a visit.
- **DEVICE**: Smartphone.

In this case, the audience needs information in small chunks to help them get to where they're going, find the people they're supposed to meet with, navigate around campus and the surrounding area, and share what they're doing with their friends and family.

An app or a well-made, responsive site optimized to provide navigational and contextual information on a small screen is the most effective means of communication for this situation. You have your audience's attention already. Now you need to convert them from prospective student to applicant.

Ad Astra Per Aspera

In Latin, *"ad astra per aspera"* translates roughly as "to the stars through difficulties" or "a rough road leads to the stars." In either case, it's an inspirational phrase that tells us we have to put up with a lot of tough stuff before we reach the heavens.

Although smartphones have been with us for well over a decade, we're only beginning to understand how these devices are impacting our culture. Are we losing touch with that value of face-to-face interactions? Are we prioritizing internet "fame" to the detriment of more meaningful achievement? Is the ability to share every moment of our lives with strangers remaking our sense of community and self? Are continuous streams of the world around us (i.e., Facebook Live), changing the way we perceive reality?

Soon, a generation who doesn't remember life without smartphones and tablets will enter the workplace. They've already started college. What does this mean for society in general and marketing in specific? We can only guess. But we can map the new territory around us and understand how it's being used.

Organic vs. Paid Search

There are two kinds of people in this world: those who want to find the answer and those who want to be told the answer. The people who want to find answers don't trust an answer unless they find it themselves. In the context of web search, these people prefer to sift through organic search results. They are not in the minority either. According to a recent Forrester Research study, organic search results are 8.5 times more likely to be clicked on than paid search.[19]

The interesting thing about the people who prefer organic search results is that, while they do want to work to answer their questions, they don't want to work too hard. Seventy-five percent of people will never make it past the first page of search results.[20] They will either pick one of the first ten options or change their search. And, with the Forrester study finding that 81% of all website traffic comes from search engines, it's crucial to optimize your website for those engines (more on that in a moment).

Search result ads, on the other hand, fill a need for people who want to be told the answer. These people figure, often correctly, that the ads are there because someone thinks the information will meet the needs of the end-user. And, if it doesn't, they can bail at no cost to them.

In the end, however, these two types of people are not absolutist about how they answer their questions. Some organic searchers click on ads; some ad clickers also click on organic search results.

Marketers should consider running both paid and organic search campaigns concurrently if there is enough in the budget to support both activities.

The Key to Organic Search: SEO

Ranking high on search engines can be a cost-effective way to generate leads and awareness. After all, it costs you nothing when a prospective student clicks on your website's link in a list of organic search results. But how can you possibly influence what results appear in a search engine like Google? The answer: SEO.

Short for search engine optimization, SEO is a series of tactics you can use to increase your website's ranking on search engines. The higher a page ranks on a search engine results page (SERP), the more clicks it gets. But the rate of dropoff as you go down the SERP is exponential. And, as we noted, most people never make it to the second page of results.

Because of how people use SERPs, you want your website and its respective pages to rank as high as possible for as many search terms as possible. But to understand how SEO tactics help you achieve that, you need to understand how search engines create their rankings. Or, more specifically, you need to understand how Google creates its rankings. The vast majority of all internet searches run through Google, making it the alpha and omega of SEO.

Not every detail of Google's ranking system is known — the company keeps many aspects private — and yet, we still know quite a bit. The most important bit is this: The rankings are an algorithm that, while designed by humans, runs with very little human influence. Instead, Google uses automated software that crawls through millions and millions of web pages, indexing information and storing it in Google's search databases. Every time someone searches for a word or phrase, Google runs the copious amounts of information its bots have indexed through its ranking algorithm and produces a SERP that provides what the algorithm thinks are the best/most useful results for the search term.

So, to improve your search engine rankings, you have to make sure that Google's algorithm sees your site as a top fit for certain terms. And that means providing Google's bots with the right kind of information in the right places. What's the right kind of information and what are the right places? Let's break it down.

In the Realm of SEO, Content Is King

The most important factor to how your website ranks is its content. Does your content fulfill a specific need? Does the content make its subject matter clear? Is it helpful to real people? Is it of higher quality than the vast majority of pages covering similar content?

If you can answer yes to all of that, your site is well on its way to being optimized. If you can't answer yes, or if you're unsure, that's OK. A lot of sites — especially older ones that haven't gone through a major update in a while — have less than optimal content. The good news is, you can create new content that is of higher quality and of more use to prospective students and other users who come to your site.

But even if your content is the absolute best it can be, there's more you can do to improve your SEO. In particular, you can ensure other text elements clearly communicate the content of each page so that Google's bots can quickly decipher what your site and its pages provide. These other text elements include:

- **TITLE TAGS:** This is the title of a page, which Google displays as the title of the search result. A good title clearly yet succinctly describes the content of the page, such as: BS in Business Management | Your University. A bad title fails to provide useful information about the content, such as: Degrees. Not only is a good title important for SEO, it makes it easier for users to decide if your page has the information they want.

- **URL:** This is the web address of a page, which should give a good sense of what the page is about and where it falls in the hierarchy of the site. A good URL would be: YourUniversity.edu/academics/bachelors-degrees/bs-business-management. A bad URL would be: YourUniversity.edu/3432910/bs321. Like title tags, Google uses URLs to help determine what a page is about *and* real people use them to help determine if the page is likely to meet their needs.

- **IMAGE ALT TEXT:** This is text that describes a photo and appears when your mouse pointer hovers over that photo. Alt text exists to help visually impaired users understand what's contained in a photo, and you should write alt text with that purpose first in your mind. But alt text also helps Google rank your web pages and your individual photos. The better and more specifically you can describe a photo, the more it will help with your search rankings. For example, the alt tag for a photo of a student on campus shouldn't be "student." It should be closer to "Male student at Your University sits under a tree, studying for a physics exam."

- **META DESCRIPTIONS:** This is the description of a page, which Google displays as the description of the search result. While Google doesn't use meta descriptions as a ranking factor, they're still highly important. Well-written meta descriptions will improve your click-through rate because they'll catch the attention of prospects. Poorly written meta descriptions, on the other hand, could make a prospect decide your university doesn't have what they're looking for. The more your meta description is written like a quality ad, the better the results you'll see.

The Power of Keywords in SEO

Content may be king, but it's not the whole SEO court. When optimizing a website, you also need to think about keywords.

Keywords are words or phrases that you include in your site because they mirror search terms commonly entered by users. Google rewards sites that have keywords that exactly match what a user has typed into the search field. The more exact matches you have, the better. But there's a big caveat.

Your university is extremely unlikely to rank at the top of the first SERP for "university" or "bachelor's programs" or any other term that could apply to every university in the nation. Common terms in any industry are highly competitive, making them costly if not impossible to rank for.

Instead of thinking generally about which search terms apply to the pages on your site, think specifically. What terms might apply to you that don't apply to many other universities but are still likely to be searched for by your target audience? For example, if you are a private Catholic school in Texas, you should focus your efforts on ranking high for terms like "Texas Catholic university," "private Catholic colleges in Texas," and similar phrases your best prospects are likely to search for.

Developing a List of SEO Keywords

Because you want to rank for as many *accurate* search terms as possible, you want to develop a long list of keywords. There are a lot of ways to do this, but the best method is to combine brainstorming with research on Google Analytics and sites like Moz and SpyFu. Ultimately, your list should include multiple iterations of everything from your school's name to the degree programs you offer to descriptions of your location and focus (e.g., "private Catholic colleges in Texas").

Nevertheless, your goal isn't to rank for every keyword you put on your initial list. Your goal is to rank high for the best of the keywords. One way to determine what the best keywords are is to run your full list through a site like Moz, which will provide you with the amount of traffic (searches) a specific keyword or keyword phrase receives in a month along with a rating that shows how difficult it is to rank for that keyword (which is a function of how many other sites are ranking for the keyword). Your goal is to find the keywords on your list that have good traffic but moderate to easy difficulty. Those are some of the best keywords for your site because those are the keywords you can, with effort, rank near the top for.

You can also rank high for long tail keywords. These keywords are longer phrases that fit your prospects' interests extremely well. They don't generate much traffic but, when they do, you can rank at the very top of the SERP and almost certainly attract the attention of the prospect who typed in the phrase. And because these prospects are searching for something so specific to your institution, they are often valuable leads. When choosing long tail keywords, you want phrases that will be an exact match to a user search, so you'll need to turn to your research to determine what longer phrases are likely to match the searches of your best prospects. For that private Catholic college in Texas, a list of long tail keywords could include "what's the best small Catholic school in the San Antonio area," "finding a good Catholic college in Texas with low tuition," and "scholarships for Catholic colleges in south and central Texas." As long as those phrases fit what the college is and what it offers, they can generate valuable leads even without generating much traffic.

Using Keywords in SEO

Once you have a list of the best keywords, you can use them strategically to improve your rankings. Anywhere you have text, you can insert keywords, which the bots will see when crawling your website.

The best places for keywords are in the title tag and in the main headline on each page (called the H1). Including them in subheads (called H2, H3, H4, etc., depending on their hierarchy) and throughout the body copy is also a good idea. In meta descriptions, Google will bold keywords that match a user's search terms. As previously noted, Google doesn't use meta descriptions in their ranking factors, but those bolded terms can help attract the attention of prospects, so it's a good idea to include a keyword or two in each page's meta description.

However, don't overuse keywords. Google's bots will detect what's called keyword stuffing and penalize your rankings. Instead, deploy keywords judiciously, using them where they make the most sense in context. If a keyword or keyword phrase seems out of place, it's best to avoid using it there. Remember, good content matters more than anything else.

Other Aspects of SEO

Experts have written entire books on SEO, making a deep dive into the topic outside of our scope. Nevertheless, the overview above should help you make significant improvements to your website and its search engine rankings. If you want to go further, here's an abbreviated list of additional tactics used by sites with exceptional SEO.

- The design is aesthetically pleasing.
- The navigation is easy to use.
- The site works well on all browsers and properly resizes for desktop and mobile.
- Pages render fast.
- Redirects from older versions of the site come direct.
- Structured Data Markup is used wherever applicable.
- Numerous, high-quality sites link to the site.
- Many social media posts link to the site.

Paid Search

While SEO can add a lot of value to your website, the cost of implementing a good SEO plan can be high. Plus, implementing effective SEO takes time. If you're looking for a less involved way to generate links — or you want to augment your SEO efforts with links guaranteed to appear at the top of a difficult-to-break-into SERP — you may want to consider paid search.

Paid search is exactly what it sounds like. You pay to have your link appear at the top of the first SERP for a specific term or set of terms. You can refine who sees your link and potentially save yourself money by limiting your link to certain user demographics and/or geographical locations. While Google will mark your link as an ad, paid search is a good way to get a link in front of the users most likely to be interested in your university.

But be warned: Paid search can be very expensive and wasteful if it's not done correctly. There are many factors to consider and regularly fine tune, a process that could make anyone's head explode. If your budget allows, the best bet is to hire a certified, honest search consultant to do the work on your behalf.

However, even with the most expert help and great lemons, you can't always make lemonade. If there is low search volume for a particular search term or phrase in your demographic and geographic target, there is little you can do to substantially increase qualified traffic to your site. You can always broaden the targeting by using looser terms or relaxing the demography/geography, but that generally results in less quality traffic, which will invariably impact your quality scores and drive up your media cost.

As with SEO, paid search can be a great addition to your traffic strategy, but it has its limits. Fortunately, the internet offers additional ways to drive prospects to your site.

Social Media

Social media has become a key component of most organizations' marketing plans, with marketers spending billions every year on social media marketing initiatives.[21] And while surveys vary as to which market segments are using social media marketing at the highest rates, it's safe to say that using social media in some capacity is now the norm across all industries.

But is it working? The February 2019 CMO Survey reports that, while total social media expenditures across all industries is on the rise, marketers are pulling back on the spending as a proportion of their overall spend, with investments declining from a high of 13.8% of marketing expenditures in August of 2018 to 11.4% in February 2019.[22] When asked whether social media marketing has contributed to their company's overall performance, CMO Survey respondents were unenthusiastic, rating social media's contribution a middling 3.3 out of a 7 point impact scale (7 indicating a "very high" contribution). Nevertheless, most still see social media as a branding tool, with 88.2% of respondents indicating that their primary use of social media is in "brand awareness and brand building," not necessarily as a direct response tool. For direct response, they're shifting their spending into paid media, with social media only accounting for about 14% of the paid media mix.

Of course, there are plenty of anecdotal examples of social media campaigns that have been hugely successful at generating leads. But for every social media success story, there are thousands of brands struggling to make social media work. When Instagram superstar @Arii can't sell 36 t-shirts to her 2.6 million followers,[23] it's pretty clear that there's a hype-gap between the promise of social media and the reality.

To understand why social media isn't working for many, we have to ask what it is that marketers are trying to do with social media. While asking 10 marketers this question will probably yield you 20 answers, the 2019 Social Media Marketing Report found that the number one objective among marketers was pretty simple: Use social media to engage with customers.[24]

Seems like common sense, right? Isn't the promise of social media that it's going to help us engage with our customers in a way that's never been possible? Aren't we doing enough if we're simply asking them to "like" or "follow" us and maybe engage in a little bit of conversation now and again? We all know that if we can get them to interact with us, they're ours, right?

Maybe not. And that's because consumers don't always form opinions in the ways we wish they did.

A study published by the Society for New Communications Research[25] found that the top five influencers of consumer attitudes were:

- Quality of products and services: 80%
- Cost: 55%
- Customer care programs: 37%
- What family, friends, and trusted people say about the company: 34%
- Customer reviews and ratings on social media sites: 30%

Adding to this is what Accenture found when they surveyed 30,000 consumers around the world (2,000 in the U.S.).[26] They discovered that the majority (62%) "want companies to take a stand on current and broadly relevant issues such as sustainability, transparency, and fair employment practices." And companies that don't do this risk paying the price. The same survey found that 42% of consumers will walk away from a brand when they're not open about their views on important social issues and 21% say that they're never coming back.

What does all this tell us? It tells us that some truths hold firm in the internet age. Consumers prize quality and consider price important.

What seems to be new is that, in addition to old standbys, consumers are increasingly evaluating brands on how well they align with their values.

What about customer service? Doesn't that play a role as well? It does. In a survey of consumers that looked at why they shop retail (rather than online), a big chunk of them said that they choose physical stores because they want access to and advice from knowledgeable sales people.[27] Unfortunately, almost three-quarters of them admit they end up frustrated because the salespeople don't seem to know anything about the products, don't know what else is in the store, and haven't the foggiest notion of what is in stock.

That would seem to open up room for companies to leverage the power of social media to provide online customer engagement and conversations that are as good as what the brick-and-mortar shoppers hope to (but don't) find offline. The problem is, even as technology allows us to gather more and more data about customer behavior, the consensus seems to be that customer service is still lousy.[28]

Successful social media marketing appears even more impossible when you narrow in on education and look at the E-Expectations Report from Noel-Levitz, which surveyed more than 1,000 high school students going through the college search process.[29] What it found is that, while college websites continue to be the most influential medium when it comes to college choice (4.09 out of 5 on their influence scale), posts on social media were reported to be the *least* influential method of communicating (2.99 out of 5). Clearly, prospective students are looking at social media, so why doesn't the social media marketing being thrown at them have any impact?

Maybe the answer can be found in examining how these students want to engage with the schools they're interested in. Overall, according to Noel-Levitz, email and texting seem to be the preferred method of communicating with schools, with 61% preferring an email response after filling out a request for information form and 67% reporting that they wanted texts during and after the application process. Couple this with the fact that 40% reported ditching RFI forms that asked for too much information, and it seems as if it's the highly personal engagement inherent in social media that's the turn-off. In fact, as a study by Pitney Bowes and the CMO Council found, Gen Z (today's prospective undergraduates) are much more concerned about data privacy than the older millennial cohort, making them suspicious of unsolicited communications.[30]

And herein lies the entire problem with social media marketing (and why many of us are doing it wrong): We want to engage with our audience, but they don't want to engage with us. Yes, they expect us to engage with them when they complain or ask us for something specific, but they're not interested in an ongoing dialogue.

So, is social media marketing a lost cause? Not at all. The National Merchants Association found that 80% of Gen Z-ers reported that social media influences their purchases.[31] Social media *can* dramatically affect what people buy; it just doesn't work as many marketers wish it did.

Take the people known as social media influencers. These are people who have managed to amass a devoted social media following. Most focus on a specific topic, like wellness or activism or food. But no matter what they're posting about, they all share one thing in common: They connect with followers in a way that few brands ever manage. And that connection can be powerful.

People tend to implicitly trust influencers they follow because they often think of them as a highly credible friend or peer. This gives an influencer's advice the power of peer-endorsement, which a 2016 marketing study showed to be a strong influence on other people's perceptions, particularly in relation to what people think about brands.[32]

Not surprisingly, some brands have caught on to this phenomenon and it's not uncommon for brands to pay or otherwise entice social media influencers to promote their brand. And these influencers don't have to be major celebrities to attract a brand's attention. Influencer endorsement is considered so powerful that micro-influencers — influencers who have 10,000 to 50,000 followers — are becoming increasingly important in influencer-driven marketing.[33] Clearly, marketers are seeing benefits from outsourcing their promotions.

But, the lesson isn't that you have to skirt ethical lines and buy the influence of others to succeed in social media marketing. The lesson is that people share things and respond to what is shared because those things serve a social purpose within a real (albeit online) community. Those doing the sharing want to form a deeper relationship with each other, not with the brand that produces a product or service. The brand is a bond within the community, but the community isn't inherently bonded to the brand.

To make social media marketing work, you have to accept the hard truth: Consumers don't want to talk to you until they want to talk to you. Trying to force the issue with ham-handed attempts at "engagement" isn't going to work. But if you can make people want to talk to each other *about* your brand, you can gain some real value from your social media efforts.

Here are seven things to think about when constructing your next social media campaign:

- **It all begins and ends with content.** Sharing happens among networks of peers because people want to share. So, give them something worth sharing. Skimping on production, creativity, and audience focus when it comes to generating content for your social media presence means that you're just wasting your time and money.

- **Make it easy to share.** If you have a website, do everything you can to make your content easy for people to share. But don't force it down their throats. Include sharing links everywhere you can, make compelling images (or infographics) that are pinnable, and create a unique hashtag that makes the content/campaign easy to reference. Whatever you can do to grease the wheels of sharing will help you get your content out there.

- **Understand that you're a small part of their world.** It might be your life, but they're not going to think about your company very often. Unless you're a major affinity brand like Apple or Disney, or a sports franchise, don't expect them to think about you until they need you. Bombarding them with irrelevant or forced content isn't going to get them to love you more.

- **Respond quickly.** Your customers will talk to you when they want to talk to you. If you're not there to respond, you're going to create some serious ill will.

- **Provide value.** Make 'em laugh. Give them something to think about. Whatever it is, it should be valuable to them and their social networks.

- **Respect privacy.** People are getting pretty savvy. You can't trick them into receiving your stuff. If they don't feel that their privacy is being protected (selling, ahem, your list, ahem, to third parties), then they'll be inclined to go away.

- **Success = sharing.** When it comes down to it, if people are sharing your stuff in their own networks, you're winning. "Likes" and "follows" don't really count. And volume isn't always a good indicator of success. Remember, micro-influencers don't have a huge volume of followers. But they do have meaningful engagement.

Social media marketing isn't tough, but many of us have been doing it all wrong. It's about conversations — just not with us.

Content Marketing

One thing that the digital marketing industry is superior at is taking old ideas and renaming them so that they seem hip and new. Think that social media is new? Folks who lived in the San Francisco Bay Area were posting messages back and forth to each other on the Community Memory system in 1973. Still trying to wrap your head around email marketing? The first use of electronic communication to send messages that advertised a service occurred in 1864 when a dentist in England sent a mass telegram to politicians advertising his services. Are your designers still trying to figure out how to create effective banner ads? AT&T placed them back in 1994, more than 25 years ago!

So, when we encounter the hype around content marketing, many of us who've been around the online block more than a few times tend to roll our eyes. After all, the ancient Roman government used newsletter-like bulletins posted around cities as a way of communicating with their people. Even if you want to strictly limit your definition of branded content to "content being used to market a company's products and services through mass-produced materials," all you have to do is check out the magazine *The Furrow*, produced by John Deere, the tractor manufacturer, to see an example of content marketing that's more than 100 years old.[34]

In other words, content marketing is not a new technique. And you can't expect it to work just because it's got a buzzwordy name. The web is littered with viral videos that weren't, and there probably isn't a single person reading this who hasn't encountered more than a fair share of ghost blogs, dead Twitter feeds, and zombie Facebook pages. Content alone doesn't lead to successful content marketing. What you need is content that's good and strategic.

But let's back up. Why do you need content marketing in the first place? Well, you don't if your other marketing efforts are raking in the qualified prospects. But if you're reading this book, it's likely that you want to give your marketing a boost. And content marketing can do just that.

Successful content marketing achieves two things at once.

1. It attracts prospects who may be less inclined to pay attention to traditional forms of marketing.

2. It clarifies/improves your brand positioning.

Content marketing can achieve those things because it comes at marketing from a unique angle. Instead of blatantly promoting a product or service, content marketing informs or entertains. If the information or entertainment fulfills an audience's needs/desires, that audience is likely to form a positive view of the brand responsible.

Some examples will help explain.

Marcus Sheridan, part owner of a fiberglass pool manufacturer, gave the world one of the most famous modern examples of good content marketing when he started a company blog during the Great Recession.[35] Unlike most company blogs of the era, he didn't post product promotions. He answered common questions people had about fiberglass pools.

Why was this good content marketing? Because of our old friend SEO. You'll remember that Google likes content that's unique and fulfills a user's need. Sheridan's blogs achieved both. Whenever someone Googled a question about fiberglass pools, one of Sheridan's blog posts would typically come up as a top result on the SERP. This drove a lot of traffic to his business *and* branded his business as a preeminent expert on fiberglass pool construction and installation. The blog didn't just save his business during the Great Recession; it set the business up for years of growth and success.

But informative blogs are just one kind of modern content marketing. In 2016, Nike produced *Margot vs Lily*, a YouTube series about two quirky millennial women.[36] While the characters often wear Nike products, the show wasn't one long product placement. Instead, it was an earnest attempt to produce a show that people would talk about and share links to. The point wasn't to scream "wear Nike!" but to help Nike position itself as a brand in tune with young, female consumers.

Did it work? It's hard to measure the effects of content marketing on an already massive and well-known brand, but young women currently rank Nike as the most innovative athletic brand,[37] which is the exact position Nike was shooting for.

Taken together, Marcus Sheridan's blog and Nike's YouTube series give a good sense of how content marketing can take a lot of forms — and require a wide range of budgets. What's right for your university will depend a lot on who your audience is, what concerns/interests/entertains them, what your budget is, and what brand image you want to project.

Nevertheless, all good content marketing starts the same way: with good content. Many content marketers go wrong because they prioritize the marketing part. But if you want to avoid wasting money on something no one will appreciate or share, you have to make something that fills a need first and makes you look good second.

Many universities publish blogs and/or produce videos that provide thought leadership or insights into their major areas of expertise. Some produce content covering a fun activity that happens to feature their students. And while we don't know of a university that has produced its own YouTube series in the vein of what Nike created, content marketing like that could conceivably work — if it's good on its own merits.

Ultimately, just like with SEO, content is king.

Measuring Your Success

Measuring the success of marketing efforts has always been a challenge. For decades, organizations have struggled to know which ads, mailers, brochures, billboards, etc. are working and thus worth the investment. With the rise of the internet, the items on the "Is it working?" list have only increased and now include emails, websites, social media posts, SEO initiatives, and more. How are you supposed to wrap your arms around all of that?

The solution: data analytics. While the internet has dramatically expanded the number of traffic-generating channels, it has also given us a bevy of new tools we can use to measure the effectiveness of those channels. And it's not as complicated of a process as the words "data analytics" may make it sound.

If you're like the vast majority of universities and other organizations, your website is where you're driving most, if not all, of your traffic, whether you're sending prospects to a specific program page, a specialized landing page, or the home page. By running analytic software in the background of your website, you can track — and measure — every visit to your site.

Many types of analytic software exist in the marketplace, but the most popular is Google Analytics. Through Google Analytics, you can run a huge variety of reports, some of which require training to master. But even the most basic functions of Google Analytics can be quite useful.

With Google Analytics, you can track:

- The number of users to your site on a daily or even hourly basis.
- How many of your visitors are new vs. returning.
- How long users stay on your site.
- User demographics, including gender, age, and geographical location.
- Where your visitors are coming from (organic search, paid ads, social media, etc.).
- What keywords users typed in to find you.
- What pages users land on and where in your site they go from there.
- What device (mobile vs. desktop) and browser visitors are using.

Within each of the basic categories of tracking, you can drill down to quite specific detail. You can even combine categories to examine specific market segments (e.g. number of new users between September and December of last year who were 18- to 24-year-old women living in Midwestern states, searching for "universities with women's basketball scholarships").

Through these analytic tools, you can measure the success of most online traffic-generating activities and even some offline ones as well (thanks to unique URLs and landing pages). The key is to know what you're looking for. To help you get started, here's a basic guide on measuring the success of different types of traffic-generating efforts:

- **OVERALL CAMPAIGN:** Did your site visits rise when the campaign started? Did visits rise among the targeted demographic group? Are the number of visits remaining elevated?

- **SEO INITIATIVE:** Are site visits via organic search going up? Are users who searched for the keywords you prioritized going up? Are visits by your target demographic going up?

- **EMAIL CAMPAIGN:** How many direct links are you getting from the email? Has overall traffic gone up?

- **SOCIAL MEDIA CAMPAIGN:** How many direct links are you getting from the social media platforms you're on? How many shares and likes are you generating (not something Google Analytics tracks, but easily discoverable through your social media page)?

- **CONTENT MARKETING:** Is the specific page hosting the content receiving the traffic numbers you hoped for and are users staying on the page? How much traffic is going from the content page to other pages on your site? Is the content being shared and/or discussed on social media?

- **DISPLAY AND PAID SEARCH:** How many click-throughs are the ads generating? Is the overall traffic to the site going up?

- **PRINT ADS:** How many users are landing on the unique URL/landing page you created for the ad? How many of those users are going to other pages on your site and/or filling out an RFI?

In many ways, analytics takes the guesswork out of what efforts are generating traffic and what efforts aren't. We strongly recommend using them as much as you can, which means running as much of your traffic through analytic-enabled websites as possible. Even when hosting an open house, you can set up a landing page for RSVPs.

In situations when traffic doesn't pass through your website (e.g. a no-RSVP open house advertised on the radio), we recommend sticking to the more old-fashioned way of measuring traffic: Count how many people responded and do your best to measure how many fit your target demographic.

Case Study:
From Digital Traffic
to Foot Traffic

Getting thousands of people to the somewhat-rural campus of our mid-sized public university client wasn't going to be easy. Far from major transportation hubs, the school suffered from a lack of awareness. To add to the challenge, our client wanted to reach out into regional metropolitan areas, particularly to groups of prospective students.

Since we had to reach out to high school students, we went where more and more of them spend their time these days: online streaming media. We chose one of the most popular free, ad-supported streaming music services because we'd been impressed with both their demographic reach and targeting abilities. We had used this partner in the past to deliver open house attendees and it was always successful. This effort was no exception.

The results were astounding. By the end of the multi-week campaign, we'd received thousands of RSVPs and had been able to direct interested students and their parents to transportation options for the one-day, campus-wide open house. When the big day came, the campus was filled with more than 2,100 attendees, eager and ready to learn more about what our client had to offer.

THE SECOND PILLAR: DESTINATION

131

All that traffic you're creating needs to lead to a destination. *Destination* **could mean an open house at your student center, a traveling open house at a hotel, a webpage promoting a particular degree program, a landing page focused on a particular action (e.g., make an appointment with an admissions counselor), or even the homepage of your website. Regardless of the particular destination, each must be designed in a way that supports your brand, message, and goals, and each must be engineered to spur further action.**

The term "destination" implies specificity. Just as you can't buy a bus ticket to "The West," your traffic can't or won't arrive without people being given a specific place to go. And once they are there, the destination has to give them something to do. The best destinations educate, refine traffic flow, and lead the prospect further toward a decision (preferably enrolling). Based on our experience, the more a destination is tailored to a specific audience and their needs, the better it works. Simply sending all your traffic to your homepage and hoping for the best is an inefficient way to generate a desired outcome (although there's a lot you can do to make your website work as a marketing tool, as we'll discuss in a moment).

In addition to optimizing your digital destinations, take care to align admissions talking points with up-to-date branding and marketing efforts. Train anyone who will interact with your audiences to make sure your messaging is second nature, and craft prompts that will help your representatives move prospects down the sales funnel (or around the sales loop, as we prefer to say).

If your destination involves live interaction in a physical place, come prepared with enough people (e.g., admissions representatives) and stuff (brochures, viewbooks, applications, etc.) to engage the people that you've driven to the location (i.e., your traffic). If you can, offer "live online" or traveling events that replace the need for prospects to come to campus. We've helped clients set up on-the-spot admissions interviews, instant-admit events, and information sessions.

And, by all means, build data collection into all destinations, such as adding Google Analytics to your websites. You can't know what's working and what's not — and adjust your marketing tactics accordingly — if you don't have the data to back up your decisions.

All that said, we realize that developing the right destinations for your audiences can be difficult. Which is why you'll find some tips below for the most common — and often most successful — types of destinations.

Your Primary Website

For most modern organizations, their website is at the center of their marketing, and often their sales operations too. There is no Amazon without Amazon.com. But it's not just tech giants who rely on their websites. Brick-and-mortar retailer Target did $5.35 billion in online sales in 2018 alone,[38] nonprofits are increasingly receiving donations online,[39] and even most government agencies have websites with online forms and permit renewals.

The role of websites in higher education is equally as vital. No doubt, your institution has one. And it's probably large, with a lot of content covering your degree programs, admissions requirements, student life, and more. The question is: Is it working as a marketing destination?

Plenty of higher education institutions have websites that are more of a repository of content than they are a usable piece of marketing. In other words, they don't engage the visitor. And when we talk about engagement, we're talking about a lot more than a snappy headline or an interactive widget. We're talking about delivering personalized content that makes your visitors feel like the website was designed for them and their interests/needs.

Delivering this kind of user experience (UX) requires good planning and good design. Whenever creating a brand new website or updating an existing one, keep the following guidelines in mind.

- **Design for the user.** Don't look at your website like a storage unit. Think of it more like a grocery store. When you go to a grocery store, you have expectations of where things will be. The more a store meets those expectations, the more enjoyable the shopping experience. Imagine being able to find everything you need without ever going down the wrong aisle. *That's* the UX you want for your website. Navigating it should feel intuitive. While that's easier said than done, it's worth the effort. Visitors who can't find what they came for will leave, but those who have a good experience are likely to connect with you or at least come back soon.

- **Create accessible, usable, appropriate content.** When a visitor finds the page they want, it's essential that the content is useful. You should know how each page within your site relates to a step in a user's journey/decision-making process and then provide the content — and only the content — that meets the needs of that step and encourages the user toward the next step. Be comprehensive without being overwhelming and thorough without being redundant. And always keep the focus on the user so that their journey through your site mirrors their journey through the decision-making process.

- **Speak in the users' voice while maintaining brand authority.**
  While your website is likely to attract a wide range of people, any
  individual page on your website will attract only a subset of visitors.
  For instance, an alumnus looking for ways to donate is highly unlikely
  to go to the undergraduate admissions page. Knowing which segments
  of your audience are most likely to use which pages allows you to create
  varied content so that each page speaks in a voice that connects with
  the user. As long as all of your pages still represent your overall brand,
  varying tone and word choice is an excellent way to personalize content
  and improve UX.

- **Design for the device.** Different devices, browsers, and network speeds
  can all impact how a website looks and functions. Your website needs to
  be responsive to all the ways someone might connect to it.

- **Test, measure, revise.** To ensure your website works like you intend, you
  have to test it. This includes tree testing the information architecture,
  UX testing the final product, and running tech checks on every link,
  form, and field. If anything isn't working, fix it before your launch or as
  soon you can afford to.

Landing Pages and Microsites

Your main website is not the only web presence you can, or should, have.
If you want to connect to a specific audience at a minimal cost, consider
building a landing page or microsite that fulfills a particular need of that
audience. Not only do these kinds of sites allow you to micro-target, they also
allow you to test innovative approaches to attracting and engaging prospects.

These sites can live on their own domain or sit within your larger website
domain. The key is that they serve as a front door to a specific audience
seeking specific information (e.g. working professionals looking for MBA
night classes in the Denver area). Search, social sharing, emails, and even
traditional marketing materials like flyers can drive the traffic you need.
But, for a landing page or microsite to be effective, it needs to meet the
audience's expectations and wants. To achieve that, we suggest taking
these steps:

- **Be everything for someone.** What does this audience segment want to see and do on the site? Give that to them. Don't water things down with secondary requirements or content that appeases an internal stakeholder more than it appeals to a prospect.

- **Define a clear call to action — and support it.** Make sure your users know what you want them to do. State the purpose of your landing page. Provide a button with a clear call to action. Add a call to action as an in-context text link, either within or at the end of a paragraph. Run a usability test. Understand that all of the content leads to and persuades the desired action.

- **Personalize forms.** Customer relationship management tables prioritize contact information over personal interests. It's more than likely that your intended audience thinks about it in reverse. Imagine having a conversation with prospects. Ask about their interests and passions, then request contact information.

- **Trim required fields.** What is the least amount of information you need to create a conversion? Is it a name and an email address? Then why require a phone number, date of birth, or zip code? Fewer required fields will yield more conversions.

- **A/B test.** If you're torn between two techniques, try both so you can run an A/B test. Track conversions for a brief period, then select the better performing option as the destination for every visitor. Everything's open for testing, including button labels, colors, and the order of content. Use your data to resolve internal debates.

Virtual Tours

Virtual tours can be a powerful way to show prospective undergrads what your campus looks like. After all, "What's it like to go there?" is one of the top questions on a prospective undergrad's mind.

But virtual tours are tricky. While they can show off your campus in a way that a website alone can't, they can also damage your brand if done poorly. Here are some things to consider when evaluating virtual tour vendors:

1. **What other work have they done?** The best way to tell if a virtual tour vendor is going to deliver on their promises is to look at previous work they've done … work that's actually on the web. We can't stress that last point enough. There's a big difference between demos created to wow prospective clients (or investors) and actual virtual tours of actual schools that are actually being used by prospects.

2. **Does all of their work look the same?** Many vendors used canned, template-ized systems to create virtual tours that all look suspiciously similar and do little to show off any particular institution's brand experience. Avoid them and avoid being sucked in by their low-cost solutions.

3. **Do they try to hide costs with "creative" cost structures?** Some fly-by-night operators like to approach you with business models that promise a low initial cash outlay followed by a licensing commitment. Don't choose this option. Models that require a low initial investment but a long-term licensing commitment with payments based on users, leads, or other variables out of your control can leave you in trouble. And ad-supported models? Forget it.

4. **Are their tours easy to use and navigate?** We don't care how old or non-techie you think you are; if you can't successfully navigate a virtual tour, your prospects are probably going to have trouble as well, even if they are digital natives. And don't forget: Their parents might want to take a look too.

5. **Is anything hidden in the fine print?** Finally, read the standard terms and conditions early in the sales process. Will your institution own the finished tour? Is pricing based on nodes (locations) included or will the job be priced for a flat fee? What about licensing and maintenance? What happens if you need a change made (e.g., a new building added to campus)? What kind of support will you receive after the virtual tour has launched? Don't be fooled by happy techie-speak. If you don't understand something, keep asking until you do.

Beyond Undergrads

While we usually think of virtual tours as undergraduate recruitment tools, they can be powerful ways of reaching out to graduate students too, especially graduate students in disciplines where locations or facilities matter. Virtual tours of labs and technical equipment can be a powerful way of reaching prospective students in STEM disciplines. For prospects interested in graduate business education, facilities such as stock trading floors, conference rooms, and even lounge/networking areas can be powerful draws. For art and design prospects, computer labs, studios, and specialized equipment can communicate more about your brand than any amount of copy ever could. Even humanities prospects can benefit from a tour around the department and areas such as libraries, reading rooms, or historical document archives and collections.

Program Finders, Tuition Calculators, and Other Interactive Elements

If you work in higher ed, it's easy to forget the intricacies of how the industry works. Variations on degree programs, the labyrinth that is financial aid, and the nitty gritty of general education can all be confusing to outsiders, especially prospective students who may have been out of school for a long time (graduate prospects) or who've never been to college (undergraduate prospects). And if they get confused while trying to figure out how your school would meet their needs, you can be sure that they're not going to be too interested in applying.

Enter interactive program explorers and calculators.

An interactive program explorer is like an expert advisor who can help direct you to the program that best fits your interests, your education level, your desired learning pace, or any other factor that goes into the decision of whether or not to apply to a school. With a program explorer, all students have to do is answer some questions about their interests and their desired format or pace and — *voilà!* — out pops a list of programs that meet their needs.

Calculators can also help prospects make a decision. While we're all familiar with the Cost of Attendance calculator, any decision that relies on quantitative data (financial aid is the obvious one) can be turned into a calculator that helps prospective students learn whether or not your school is a right fit.

Because these tools are so useful, you can easily turn them into ad-driven destinations that move prospects toward your site. Even better, because prospects have to provide answers to the questions — many of which are pretty probing — you can use these tools to gather valuable information on your prospective students, which you can then use for everything from tailoring your program offerings to optimizing your advertising and marketing efforts.

When thinking about creating an interactive tool destination, keep in mind a few things:

1. **Make it useful for the prospect.** If your tool isn't useful, people aren't going to use it.

2. **Collaborate on the construction.** To be useful, these tools have to incorporate knowledge from a wide range of people. Creating them collaboratively — rather than in a silo — can be the difference between creating a useful tool and creating a nifty tech demo that nobody uses.

3. **Don't over-promise.** Be clear about what your tool can and cannot do. Don't promise that it's going to magically give prospects the path to their dream job if it's just going to return a list of programs you're currently pushing.

4. **Don't put up too many barriers.** Requiring prospects to go through a complex registration process before using your tool is a non-starter. Resist the urge to put up barriers and save your information gathering (beyond their answers, of course) until they're closer to wanting to request information.

Providing prospects with a tool that allows them to personalize the information they receive about your school can be a powerful engagement method as well as an easy way to have an offer you can use to attract prospects through advertising. And the more useful the tool, the more benefits you'll see.

Gated Content

From the baker's dozen to timeshare companies that will put you up in a "resort" at no cost if you listen to their sales pitch, the "free gift" as a marketing tactic is everywhere. But can the concept work for higher education? Absolutely.

The key to using free gifts — what the marketing industry calls premiums — is figuring out what gift will entice your audience but will also be inexpensive for you to provide. The solution for many colleges and universities is to offer the number one thing people turn to higher education for: knowledge.

If you want to increase the number of prospects who fill out an RFI, submit an email address, or take a similar step, offering free educational content can be a successful tactic. Because this content can only be unlocked with an action like submitting a form, it's known as gated content, and it's a specialized kind of destination.

Your gated content could be a webinar, lecture series, white paper, or any other educational material you can easily produce (or already have available). The exact content you choose should meet the interests of whatever audience segment you want to entice. It should also be good content. While prompting a prospect to take a specific action is one of the purposes of gated content, another purpose is to demonstrate the quality of the education you have to offer.

Gated content should feel special and be useful. It's not just an extra donut or a free stay in some resort. It's an experience. The better that experience, the more likely it is that a prospect will move from casual curiosity to serious interest in your institution.

Open Houses/In-Person Events

While most school's engagement with prospects happens via the internet, nothing beats speaking to prospects face-to-face. In-person events give prospects the chance to interact with you in a way that's not possible online, allowing them to have their most pressing questions answered in real-time while experiencing your institution's brand in-person. At the same time, you get the opportunity to read their body language and work your persuasive charm to guide them closer to a decision to apply.

Of course, everyone already knows that in-person contact is powerful. The real issue is getting prospects to attend an event. So, let's look at how you can improve attendance and maximize an event's benefits. We'll start with the five-stage process you'll want to follow.

1. Make prospects aware of the event.

2. Persuade them to register.

3. Do what you can to get them to attend.

4. Wow them at the event.

5. Follow up after the event to keep the momentum going.

Typically, when it comes to events, most of the energy gets spent on step number four, the event itself. But we won't focus on that. Not that the event isn't important — it is — but it's not our bailiwick and, even if it was, there's nowhere near enough space in this book to go through the basics of event planning. We'll stick to the marketing stuff: steps one, two, three, and five.

Building Awareness

Building awareness of your event is a classic marketing/communications problem. However, you can follow the tactics we've already discussed in the traffic chapter. Just remember that, while the event is the ultimate destination, the real purpose of the traffic is to drive people toward registration.

Registration

In many ways, building a good registration destination isn't much different than building any good landing page. Nevertheless, there are some differences. Specifically, your registration page should address the following:

1. **Give prospects a reason to attend.** This is the first and most important part of convincing people to register. Why should anyone come to your event? How is it going to be more useful than simply communicating with you online? If you're going to persuade someone to give up an evening for you, you need a hook that offers them something they can't get anywhere else. Some ideas include:

   A. **Instant admit: Have admissions people on hand to offer admissions on the spot, at least provisionally.** If you're going to do this right, make sure you let people know what they need to bring with them (e.g., unofficial transcripts) in order for your people to make a decision.

   B. **Free application: Offer to waive the application fee for anyone that attends your event.** They won't be able to fully complete the application at the event unless they're extraordinarily prepared, but you can get them started.

   C. **Guest speakers: High-profile speakers can be a big draw.** This can be combined with other tactics (instant admit, free application) to make the event even more attractive.

   D. **Free advice: You have a lot of expertise on your campus.** Put it to use by offering free career counseling, free transfer credit evaluations, or free sit-downs with faculty or advisors who can help prospects match their goals to your offerings.

2. **Be clear about the event's where, when, and how.** If you're putting on an event, make sure you're beyond clear about when (time and date) and where (address) the event is. Include at least some basic info on how to get to the event, including how to use public transit. If buildings on your campus don't have obvious street addresses, make sure you tell prospects how to navigate from parking to the event itself.

3. **Make it easy to take your info beyond the registration page.** Include features on your site that allow users to print a nicely formatted version of the page, import the event into their calendars, or forward the information to themselves via email or social media.

4. **Encourage sharing.** Prospects who arrive at the registration page might want to invite other people. Make it easy for them to share the event with others using social sharing buttons. You might even want to give them the ability (after registering, of course) to share an announcement that they're attending on their social media platforms of choice.

5. **Make it easy to register.** Don't require anything more than basic fields such as name, email address, and maybe some indication of what degree or subject matter they're interested in. The fewer fields, the more likely it is that a prospect will fill out your form.

Get Them to Attend

Believe it or not, attending your event isn't the most important commitment your prospects have made in their lives. Make sure to continue to nurture the budding relationship after registration with email reminders tailored to their interests (if applicable). As the event gets closer, encourage them to RSVP in order to get a more accurate headcount.

Follow-Up

After the event has concluded, please follow up! And don't just add attendees to your usual prospect email flow. Your communications should acknowledge the fact that they attended and should provide them with information that's relevant in that context. If you had a big speaker, send a link to a video or a transcript of the keynote address. If they sat down with someone for advice, send an email from that person thanking them for the chat and asking them if they have any follow-up questions. If you had an event where prospects could apply for free, make sure they get in the admissions pipeline for regular contact until they complete their application.

Events can be powerful tools to engage prospects, but only if you cover all your bases. The event itself is just one part of the entire process of building or strengthening a relationship with your prospects. This isn't just a destination; it's another step in the journey.

Best Practices for Collecting Prospect Info (RFIs and Other Techniques)

Let's be honest about what the great hope of marketing in the Digital Age really is: learning who exactly is coming to our destinations, what they do when they get there, what they really want, and how best to persuade them that our institution is the right one for their educational needs. That's not too much to ask, is it?

Well, it is, especially in today's increasingly privacy-sensitive climate. As much as we would like the name, home address, email address, phone number, social media account info, and interests of everyone who visits our websites, we're not going to get it. In fact, the more we try to get it, the less we're going to end up with.

So, how do you get the information you need? If you've read through this section, you already know part of the answer: gradually, by offering a reasonable exchange for people's information and combining that with information from other interactions, preferably in a CRM. But that's just the broad strokes. If you want actionable, specific advice, here's what we've learned about the best methods for gathering information from your destinations:

1. **Put yourself in their shoes.** Think about your own online behavior. What makes you give up valuable personal information? We bet you typically give up that information when you believe you're getting something that's valuable to you. Maybe it's a whitepaper based on proprietary research. Maybe it's access to a tool that helps you figure out something you couldn't have figured out otherwise. Maybe it's some advice that will help you get to where you want to go. Whatever the specifics, the point is: You're only going to give up your personal information in exchange for something you believe is valuable. Your prospects aren't any different.

2. **Less is more.** The truth is: The simpler the form, the greater the number of people who will fill it out. Building a relationship with a prospect is no different than building a relationship with any other human being. Nobody is going to spill their guts (and their social security number) on a first date. Don't expect your prospects to do so either.

3. **Make your calls to action obvious.** Nobody likes hunting for what they're supposed to do. As the title of the famous book on usability by Steve Krug declares, "Don't make me think." If someone has to hunt around for the button that takes them to the next step, they're going to leave.

4. **Keep them at your destination until you've gotten what you want.** While it may be tempting to include links to your main site from your landing page, don't do it. If you send prospects away, they most likely won't come back. In instances when you don't want to provide too much text on any one page but still want prospects to have access to more information, use design elements like accordions or tabs to provide detailed information. You want to focus your prospects' attention so you can intrigue them enough that they fill out your form.

5. **A picture can really be worth 1,000 words.** So can a video. The younger the prospect, the more likely they'll respond to visual content. This isn't ageism or Gen Z stereotyping. This is a fact. Visual — rather than textual — information can be much more appealing than a "wall of text" (and that's how they see it) to younger prospects.

6. **Ditch the "apply now" buttons.** We realize this might be somewhat controversial, but asking people to apply when they've just responded to an ad that leads to a landing page isn't smart. They're not there yet.

7. **Encourage sharing.** The decision to spend the kind of money it costs to enter a degree program is rarely made in a vacuum. Most of the time (and all of the time if you're marketing to traditional undergraduates), these decisions involve others such as parents, spouse/partners, or bosses. Make it easy for your prospects to include others in the conversation … they're going to anyway.

8. **Design matters.** Attractive, engaging destinations get used more than unattractive, boring ones. Design really does matter, and it's worth investing in.

9. **Test, test, test.** Repeat after us: "I am not my target market." Why? Because you aren't. There's no substitute for testing your destination on real prospects to see if you're doing something that's going to appeal to them.

Case Study:
Content Strategy Discovery

One constant we've recognized over the years is that most website redevelopment projects run into trouble when it comes to one element: content. Everything else — design, development, production — might go on without a hitch, but as soon as it's time to "feed the beast" and put content into the site, it's easy for things to go sideways.

Believe it or not, some of the most significant content problems come from established websites. There's a good reason for this: Most institutions aren't structured to be publishers. Even if a school has a division dedicated to publishing, the people hired for most administrative tasks didn't get their jobs because of their ability to publish content. And when they're charged with creating content, it's usually a task for "when they have time." Which they don't.

Nevertheless, people who aren't considered content experts have probably been tasked with producing content at your institution for a long time. Considering the state of most hallway bulletin boards and quad kiosks we see at our partner schools, producing content doesn't seem to be a problem. The issue is publishing information on the web.

This was the situation we found ourselves in when we were hired by a major health sciences campus in the South. While the campus certainly didn't suffer from a lack of communication, making the transition to the web had been tough. Like many schools, this one had decided that the web was technology and technology stuff belonged in the IT department.

A small web team, consisting of fewer than ten hard-working folks in the information technology department, managed tens of thousands of web pages. They worked valiantly to keep the content flood at bay. With a few exceptions — one school on the campus seemed to have a somewhat functional content-publishing structure — everything that had to go on the website had to flow through these folks.

While this may have been a workable approach a decade ago, it had become untenable. Few people on campus were happy, and nobody knew what to do. That's when they called us.

We knew that in order to solve their problem we had to learn everything we could about how content was created, trafficked, and published on their website. And we had to understand what kinds of expectations were in place, how the various professional schools on the campus dealt with content destined for the web, and how the process had worked up until the point we arrived.

First, we talked to people. Lots of people. Over the course of two days, we interviewed everyone responsible for web content along with the school's senior leadership, so we could discover their priorities and uncover how web content fit into the larger campus strategic direction.

In addition to conducting interviews, we also led the current web team and content creators through a series of workshops. We helped uncover their mental models for content creation so they could understand the impact of their content on the campus website.

We followed that up by collaborating with the web team to develop a new plan of action and a process that would help distribute content management throughout the entire institution. Since content management would be an additional responsibility for most content creators, we made education a big part of our plan. If people didn't know what to do, the important work wouldn't get done.

At the end of the engagement, we delivered three things that came directly from our research into content management practices:

- Recommendations for a structure that would support distributed sustainable content management.

- Recommendations for additional personnel to support the new way of distributing content responsibilities.

- Educational materials delivered as a "how to write for the web" Wiki that could serve as the foundation for the initial changes they had to make and an ongoing resource designed to support long-term change.

THE THIRD PILLAR: NURTURE

"Nurture" means to care for and encourage growth, which is what the nurture pillar is all about. After your destinations collect leads, you have to nurture those leads through the process of applying, accepting, and enrolling. And, if you subscribe to the loop, as seen in the "Defining Your Audience" chapter, your nurture activities will continue through graduation and beyond.

We call this tactic nurture rather than "push" because you can't force anyone to move from initial interest all the way through enrollment and into lifetime engagement. You can only create the conditions that make the process encouraging and simple. The prospect is in control. We are merely the friendly guides.

And yet, that doesn't mean we should be passive. When on a journey, people appreciate frequent guidance. Think about a road trip: Even if you're using a map, you rely on road signs to reassure you that you're headed the right way. If those signs aren't frequent enough, you're likely to worry that you're lost.

Don't let your prospects get lost on their journey. It's unlikely they'll stop and ask for directions. Instead, they'll just head toward a different university.

The Keys to a Successful Nurture Campaign

Compared to the first two pillars, the nurture pillar may seem simple. In some ways, that's true. Nurture campaigns don't require big investments in ad buys or website production. Instead, the bulk of a nurture campaign will happen with emails and other direct communications. But that doesn't mean they can be taken lightly.

While most direct communications are relatively inexpensive, they do take a lot of time and attention. As everyone in higher ed knows, only a percentage of the people who connect with your university will become a student. If you give the proper time and attention to a nurture campaign, you can increase the percentage who ultimately enroll by decreasing the number of prospects who drift away because they're unsure if your university is the right choice and/or don't know what steps to take.

To conduct an effective nurture campaign, you should:

- **Follow up quickly.** There is plenty of evidence that supports the obvious: The faster you follow up with prospects, the better your chances are of converting them. If they reach out to you, respond to them as quickly as you can with the information they need. These days, this means not only monitoring your phone, regular mail, and email, but also monitoring your social media channels.

- **Pay attention to timing.** Knowing to follow up when prospects contact you is one thing; but how do you know when to reach out to prospects if it's been a while since they reached out to you? The exact answer varies depending on what stage of the process they're in and where you are in your university year (i.e., whether deadlines are approaching), but you shouldn't leave the "when to reach out" question to guesswork. Instead, you should develop a schedule for when you connect to what kinds of prospects at what stage. You may be able to design much of this schedule around the seasons (application deadlines, acceptance deadlines, etc.) or you may have to conduct research to determine what works best for your audience and institution. The goal is for the pacing of your messaging to feel comfortable to your prospects so they never feel lost but don't feel bombarded either.

- **Be clear in your messaging.** Every communication of your nurture campaign should have a purpose. Simply saying "Hey, how are you doing?" will get you nowhere. Instead, use each message as an opportunity to guide prospects to the next step in their journey. And always include a clear call-to-action.

- **Multi-track messaging.** Not every prospect follows the same path from expressing interest to enrollment. Your nurture campaign should plan for that reality and develop messaging along multiple tracks. For example, some prospects may enroll immediately after being accepted. Some may not enroll until after hearing from other universities and some, even after they've heard from every university, may still hesitate to make a decision. For the first prospect, you can start communicating with them about what to do/expect now that they're enrolled. For the second, you may want to follow up the acceptance letter with an encouraging reminder that you really want them as a student (and a CTA to enroll). For the third, you may have to send the reminder and then follow up again with a message extolling the virtues of your institution and offering assistance on any issue that might be keeping them from enrolling. The more you're prepared for the different paths prospects will take, the better results you'll see. Of course, to manage all this, you may want a CRM (which we discuss below).

- **Use appropriate channels.** We've talked a lot about the many communication channels available in the Digital Age. The nurture process has to be just as acutely aware of how modern audiences use these channels as is any other part of your campaign. Often, an email is a great way to reach out. But nurture campaigns can also use text messaging, social media, postal mail, and even the telephone. Learn what works best for which prospects and at which stages.

- **Think bigger for bigger problems.** Most of your nurture communications will be short. But if you're having a particularly difficult time moving a certain audience from one step to another, you may need to think about producing a longer piece of communication. As an example, let's say you're experiencing a big dropoff between the number of MBA students you accept and the number of MBA students who enroll. After a little research, you determine that most of those who aren't enrolling are worried that they can't afford the program. Instead of simply creating a post-acceptance nurture email with some funding ideas, you should consider producing a packet (mailable and/or ebook) that explains the funding options in depth and guides students through the process of obtaining that funding. The piece could also include well-sourced information on how an MBA can pay off down the road. By thinking bigger and creating a piece of communication that answers complex questions, you can help eliminate major roadblocks for your prospective students.

- **Keep it personal.** While you'll want to use templated messages in your nurture campaign to save time and money, you'll also want those messages to feel like they're meant specifically for the recipient. You can create most of this personalized feel by sending the right messages at the right time. Creating the rest is a matter of using the friendliest and most encouraging tone within your brand style and including a personalized response to any specific question a prospect may have.

CRMs for Higher Education

A customer relationship management system (CRM) isn't anything magical; it's simply a database that allows you to gather information about interactions with prospects, students, and alumni. As you gather this information, you can build a comprehensive profile of each person in the database, including every interaction your institution has had with that person. The result is a kind of institutional memory that doesn't rely on the (often fallible) memories of people and can allow anyone who interacts with a student, prospect, or alumnus to (theoretically) recall every interaction they've ever had with the institution. Students, prospects, and alumni become much more than just numbers; they become people with histories. You can't have a relationship with a number, but you can have a relationship with a person.

CRMs also facilitate communications by allowing you to connect with people on a much more personalized level. You can load communication templates into a CRM (emails, snail mail letters, etc.) with defined variables that can be filled in by the CRM when the communication is sent and/or add conditional rules for inserting or removing content based on who the communication is being sent to. It's a quantum leap beyond the old-school mail merge that allowed simple customization. With a CRM, you can tailor what you send to the specific history of the recipient. Even better, you can log each communication in the CRM, allowing you to record the history of all your contacts, provided that staff are trained to log touches that don't go through the system, such as telephone calls or in-person meetings.

In addition to allowing you to track and nurture your prospects, students, and alumni, CRMs also offer a powerful way to build deep and lasting relationships within the campus community. When students and alumni call, they can be sure that the person at the other end will know their history with the institution. Similarly, prospects will feel that they're being welcomed into the campus community because, when they call or send an email, the person at the other end will already know what's occurred in the relationship prior to the current interaction.

Perhaps the most powerful aspect of a CRM, however, is the data that it gives marketers like you access to, especially over time. Since everything moving through the system is logged, you can use data mining techniques to gain valuable insight into what kinds of communications elicited the responses you wanted and which didn't. You'll be able to track success metrics, such as conversions, and better understand why some prospects decide to enroll and others don't. If you really want to get fancy with your CRM, you can integrate it with a web platform and use the data you gather to deliver online experiences customized to those who have visited before.

CRMs can be expensive — many require a total investment in the low-to-mid six figure range — but the investment is one with tangible results. Benefits include being able to immediately tweak your marketing communications, improving retention over the long-term, and increasing efficiencies in a whole host of campus systems, such as housing, student life, financial services, alumni relations, and more.

Case Study:
Integrated Nurture

During the late fall of 2015, a highly respected private college in the Northeast region asked us to generate leads and nurture applicants to their graduate school programs. Despite a limited budget and compressed timeline, we worked quickly to develop a brand platform, a creative strategy, and a landing page to launch shortly after the new year.

We knew that prospects who travel to campus are more likely to convert into applicants, so we recommended that our client host an on-campus open house in April. Based on the success of previous open houses, the institution challenged us to secure 100 registrations for the event, knowing that only 40% to 60% of registrations would actually attend.

Challenge accepted.

We worked with our client's marketing team to develop a digital media strategy that included the use of remarketing, digital radio, interstitials, banner ads on strategic digital partners, LinkedIn sponsored updates, LinkedIn InMails, and digital billboards along high-traffic routes. We also facilitated a robust outreach campaign to GRE test-takers, current undergraduates, alumni, and former prospects who hadn't applied to the university. We knew that combining outreach to those who were new to the institution with an appeal to those who knew the school well would help us reach the right audiences and promote word-of-mouth interest.

The results were staggering. We shattered records and delivered a total of 248 open house registrations and 125 attendees. The university's faculty and program directors were impressed enough that they went out of their way to thank our client's marketing team for delivering so many qualified prospective students. And, if you've been in higher ed marketing for a while, then you know there's no higher praise than faculty approval of your work.

LOOKING FORWARD: WHERE DATA-DRIVEN MARKETING IS LEADING

159

One of the big reasons that online advertising took off was the promise that it was trackable. Rather than just throwing ads into the broadcast void, advertisers would now know exactly how many times their ad was seen and — try to contain your excitement — how many people actually clicked on the ad to go to their site. It was a revolution in advertising, bringing resolution to John Wannamaker's old complaint: "Half the money I spend on advertising is wasted; the trouble is I don't know which half."

Now we would know exactly which half was being wasted.

Unfortunately, we weren't able to enter the promised land of advertising so easily. There were several big problems:

1. **Nobody wanted to click on banner ads (and they still don't).**
   The average "click-through rate" (CTR) — the percentage of people who see an ad and click on it — currently hovers at around 0.35% for a standard display ad.[40] In other words, for every 1,000 people who see a banner ad, only about four click on it (we're being generous and rounding up). And considering that the current conversion rate for a landing page is 2.35%,[41] you would have to buy about 12,000 impressions of your banner ad in order to land one conversion.

2. **Display ads proved to be a poor creative canvas.** The standard banner size is 468 pixels long and 60 pixels high. In the late 1990s, when SVGA monitors (800×600 pixel resolution) were the norm, a banner took up about half the user's screen. Today, when monitors average around 1920 x 1080 on laptops,[42] a banner only takes up about a quarter of the screen, providing very little space to get your message across.

3. **Banner blindness became common.** Because publishers quickly worked to standardize ad placement (top of the screen, in the menu bar on the right side of the screen, etc.), people quickly learned to not see banners because they knew where they were going to appear. This led to some truly horrific ad formats such as pop-up ads, auto-playing animated ads with sound, and just about every other obnoxious distraction advertisers could dream up. Sadly, many of these formats continue to this day.

4. **The data wasn't all that worthwhile.** Sure, you might know which ads "worked" and which didn't, but, in the beginning, that's all you knew. When cookies came into the picture, it became a lot easier to track a prospect from the first ad impression all the way to your site and to conversion, but privacy concerns led to the stripping out of personally identifiable information, leaving us with relatively useless data. Yes, you could use the performance of your ads to tweak your campaigns in real-time, but…

5. **…getting the most out of banner ads required a heck of a lot of work.** While it was theoretically possible to swap out underperforming creative, most advertisers didn't do it because real-time tracking and on-the-fly creative development required substantial resources. And, even then, a lot of publishers and ad networks didn't allow you to go in and monkey with the creative at will. Many still don't allow it.

6. **Buying online advertising was also a lot of work.** Initially, publishers and other advertising-supported sites sold their ad inventory themselves and ads were hard-coded into the pages where they were displayed. It was a lot of work for any publisher to maintain, even if they were large and well-financed. Eventually, ad networks developed, ad-serving technology matured, and it became a lot easier for everyone. But it's still a lot of work.

7. **Many advertisers didn't know what to do with the trickle of traffic their advertising generated.** It was common to send those who clicked your ad to your homepage where the user was expected to fend for themselves. Landing pages designed to capture user data came along soon enough, but it's still not terribly uncommon to see ads that point to a homepage.

Despite all the problems, the dot-com bubble swelled, fortunes were made, advertising budgets shifted to the web, and the future, it seemed to many, was going to be advertising-supported. But, the advertisers and publishers weren't so sure.

While some people were making money, many advertisers were deeply disappointed by the results they were seeing, and many publishers 1) didn't know how to deal with the new digital reality (see newspapers, if you can still find one); 2) didn't know how to sell online advertising to their long-time base of print advertisers; 3) didn't know how to price their ad inventory; 4) didn't know how to report results to advertisers or offer them any counsel on how to improve their results; and 5) didn't know what to make of the fact that, while their publication may have been one of two or so players in their respective markets before the web, once they went online, they were one of many thousands of competing publications. Major print publications in the U.S. felt forced online and watched profits shrink as they were also forced to add staff and technology in order to make the shift to the web. Many didn't make it far into the new millennium.

Then along came Google.

We're not going to recount the history of Google here, but it's important to note that Google swept in with several major innovations that changed the way we advertise.

1. **Search engine results were based (loosely and with a still closely guarded algorithm) on site popularity rather than on how well a site matched the string of words users typed into the search box.** We've already discussed how Google derives its rankings, but it's important to note that their method made it easier for people to find businesses/organizations that they were interested in and, in the process, changed how marketers thought about and used websites.

2. **Ads were minimalist and text-based, displayed (at least at first) in a clearly delineated area at the top of the page and served up based on what a user was searching for.** It's difficult to overstate the importance of this innovation for advertisers. Rather than trying to interrupt a user with image-based ads (i.e., display ads), ads on Google appeared in an organic way that made them relevant to the user. While some grumbled, consumers were pretty happy with this new way of advertising. Finally, they saw ads that not only pertained to their interests, but were useful.

3. **Advertising costs were based on an auction model and were priced based on performance, not whether or not they were displayed.** Rather than using a fixed rate card, Google priced its ads based on demand for the keyword or phrase that someone wanted to buy for their ad. Advertisers could now bid on keywords and, the more they paid, the more likely their ad was going to be seen by their target audiences. Better yet, instead of paying for an ad to be displayed, advertisers only paid when someone clicked on their ad, a model that was far more efficient than any other advertising method in existence at the time.

4. **Self-service was the name of the game.** Rather than having to go through advertising agencies, individual publishers, or ad networks, Google's advertising system was entirely self-service and included tools that helped novice advertisers pick the words that worked best for them. Additionally, Google reported results in real-time and advertisers could tweak creative on the fly — a fairly easy thing to do because the ads were all text-based. When Google Analytics launched in 2005 and integrated the Google advertising platform with site analytics, the dream of using data from ad-to-sale finally became a reality, at least for eCommerce sites.

Over time, Google expanded their ad platform to include serving display ads and text ads on sites across the web, allowing publishers to become part of the network simply by setting up an account and dropping some code on their site. Not only did this open up advertising as a viable revenue stream for millions of small publishers, but it also allowed Google to gather lots of data about user behavior. And they didn't use that data to just target ads. They sold it to advertisers, marketers, manufacturers, political campaigns, and anyone else who wanted to know what people did online.

However, Google wasn't the only innovator. The next big evolution in data-driven advertising came when Facebook opened its doors to the general public in in 2006, creating the ability to collect not only performance data about users — what sites they went to, what they looked at, what they bought, etc. — but data on *all* aspects of users' lives, including who their friends were, what bands they liked, what brands they followed, where they fell on the political spectrum, their age, gender, relationship status, etc. In other words, Facebook delivered the Holy Grail that marketers had been waiting for since the earliest days of advertising.

Other social media channels soon surged to popularity (Instagram, SnapChat, Twitter, etc.) and added even more texture to the kinds of data that could be collected. For the first time, there were sites that could collect visual data in the form of image recognition and tagging. They could even collect data about our conversations, listening to us through our social media mobile apps and, nowadays, through our televisions, personal digital assistants, smart speakers, and all other connected devices in our lives.

Through this ability to collect data, we have become the real product of the Digital Age.

So, what about privacy?

While the vast amounts of data collected about us through connected devices, cookies, and other online tracking tools offers amazing new opportunities for marketers, these opportunities have come at a cost. The 2016 presidential election made the impact of all this data collection clear when firms like Cambridge Analytica, along with political organizations and even foreign nations, used data about U.S. voters to create sophisticated influence campaigns designed to sway voters. Suddenly, our data had become a weapon for those who had the money and/or technical skill to exploit it. While we've all enjoyed the benefits of platforms like Google and Facebook, the downsides of these technologies have become clear.

Nobody can turn back the clock and return to a time before privacy became a somewhat abstract and out-dated concept. But, as marketers, we can do our part to help keep exploitation at bay, at least a little bit. And we can begin by following a few simple guidelines:

1. **Be transparent.** This isn't completely optional anymore after the EU passed laws requiring that site visitors be notified if they're being tracked with cookies. But complying with those laws should be just a first step. Ethical advertisers should take great pains to be transparent about the data we're collecting and how it's being used; and transparent in a way that's a lot friendlier than having users agree to terms of service or other such agreements they're never going to read. Be clear about what data you're collecting, how you're going to use it, and what you're going to do with it.

2. **Educate yourself and others.** It's very easy to get caught up in the gee-whiz of new technology and be lured by the siren song of infinite data about your users and prospects. Believe us, we know. But making an informed decision about whether you want to use a new technology requires understanding how that technology works and how it can be used and misused. Take the time to educate yourself about data-driven marketing technologies and teach that knowledge to others. The more we all know, the better decisions we'll make.

3. **Think critically.** Do you really need to gather all the data you're gathering? What could happen if it fell into the wrong hands? What are the limits of where you're willing to go? What safeguards do the vendors you're considering have in place to protect the data they're going to gather? Can you trust them to use it in a way that's ethically consistent with your institution's position? Are there alternatives you haven't considered yet?

Artificial Intelligence: The Next Big Thing (that's probably going to be bigger than we can imagine)

There's a lot of data out there. How much? According to research done by the World Economic Forum,[43] every day across the world:

- 500 million tweets are sent.
- 294 billion emails are sent.
- 4 petabytes of data are created on Facebook.
- 4 terabytes of data are created from each connected car.
- 65 billion messages are sent on WhatsApp.
- 5 billion searches are made.

And, they add, "By 2025, it's estimated that 463 exabytes of data will be created each day globally — that's the equivalent of 212,765,957 DVDs per day."

This is a staggering amount of data. If you consider that scholars have estimated that, at its height, the Library of Alexandria contained about 100 gigabytes of data (100,000,000,000 bytes),[44] by 2025, the world will be producing almost *5 million times* as much data as was contained in the ancient world's greatest library, every single day.

Talk about information overload! What's a human to do?

Enter artificial intelligence.

The concept of artificial intelligence — defined for our purposes as computer programs that mimic aspects of human thinking — isn't new. Greek mythology included Talos, an automaton that patrolled the shores of Crete to ward off pirates, and countless novels and speculative essays over the years have raised the idea of machines that think.

Artificial intelligence as a computing concept can be traced back to a workshop held at Dartmouth College in 1956 where computer luminaries Allen Newell (Carnegie Mellon University), Herbert Simon (CMU), John McCarthy (Massachusetts Institute of Technology), Marvin Minsky (MIT), and Arthur Samuel (IBM) created some of the first programs that learned. Early applications focused on simple tasks like playing checkers, speech synthesis, and solving algebra word problems. They were so impressed by their initial progress that Minsky predicted that, "Within a generation ... the problem of creating 'artificial intelligence' will substantially be solved."[45]

It turns out that ol' Marvin was a tad optimistic. While AI has gotten pretty sophisticated since 1956, we're a long way from any machine that comes close to thinking like a person or, in the lingo of the field, an Artificial General Intelligence (AGI). Instead, what we have is an increasingly large array of Artificial Narrow Intelligence (ANI) implementations: programs that do a fantastic job of performing in human-like ways within very narrow domains such as understanding speech, recognizing faces, driving cars, diagnosing illness, or optimizing advertising campaigns. In many cases, ANI applications can actually outperform humans for the task they've been given because of their ability to process vast amounts of data very quickly and learn from what they process. But they're still a long way from thinking in the way we conceive of humans as thinking.

Applications of AI

Even if we are a ways off from machines that think like humans, artificial intelligence is transforming our world. Computers' ability to process the ever-growing tsunami of data and learn from that data to become more effective has led to an explosion in automating not just physical tasks but intellectual tasks as well. Here are just some of the ways AI is transforming the world:

- **HEALTHCARE**: automated diagnosis and surgery, customer service, robotic patient care.

- **AUTOMOTIVE**: driverless cars, autopilot systems, intelligent safety systems that react automatically to conditions.

- **FINANCIAL SERVICES**: fraud detection, securities trading, automated compliance monitoring, financial management and decision-making, auditing.

- **GOVERNMENT**: surveillance, fraud detection.

- **ENTERTAINMENT**: video game bots, music and image generation, film editing, special effects, robots.

- **ADVERTISING**: campaign optimization, identifying market segments, predicting consumer behavior.

- **MILITARY**: semi-autonomous weapons, autonomous surveillance drones/robots, decision support systems, facial recognition and target acquisition.

AI for Marketers

So what does all this mean for you as a marketer? Right now, unless you have the resources to hire dedicated data scientists and AI developers, your ability to deploy AI in your marketing mix will have to be focused on a few main categories:

- **MARKETING AUTOMATION**: This is the most obvious application for anyone reading this (provided that Artificial General Intelligence hasn't arisen and taken over the world). Companies such as Adobe and Marketo have developed systems that use a combination of digital marketing tactics (email, social media marketing, search marketing), analytics, and an AI engine that automates many of the tedious tasks associated with managing digital campaigns, effectively reducing costs and improving performance.

- **TARGETING/SEGMENTATION:** AI's ability to sift through vast amounts of data in order to identify patterns makes the technology perfect for identifying leads, developing better market segmentation, and delivering messaging targeted at those markets. Vendors such as Digital Alchemy and Infer provide systems that use data mining, predictive modeling, machine learning, and other AI techniques to home in on new customer segments. Other tools, such as those from Zalster, help develop better segmentation *and* media planning too.

- **MARKET RESEARCH/TESTING:** While many marketing automation tools include A/B testing, it's worth noting that AI can be used to test campaign creative even if you're not going to use a full-scale marketing automation suite. Some vendors, such as Suzy, use AI to provide self-service creative testing, eliminating the need for focus groups and other "analog" testing techniques.

- **CHATBOTS/CUSTOMER SERVICE AUTOMATION:** One of the most useful new developments in AI revolves around automation of customer service, both on the phone and via text or online chats. Automated chatbots can be configured to perform many of the routine tasks humans used to do, including everything from answering student inquiries through your website or your social media properties, guiding students through the application process, or even serving as virtual teaching assistants (e.g. Georgia Tech's Jill Watson).

As we write this in the early days of 2020, there's no doubt that AI is poised to make some huge changes in the world of marketing, especially for major brands with the resources to use it. And while AI solutions for those on a budget might currently be limited to chatbots and testing, we fully believe that more widespread (and affordable) marketing AIs will be well within the reach of nearly all institutions sooner rather than later.

CONCLUSION

171

So, Where Do You Go from Here?

We know our audience, so we know not everyone who reads our book will know how to slip free of current realities and embrace the OpenEDU Model. If that applies to you and your institution, let us offer one piece of advice on getting started: Just go do it.

Step back from the short-term goals, the politics, and performance demands swirling around you and take the time to look at the big picture of what you're doing. We're not saying ignore the other matters — we know you can't — but don't let them stop you from applying the OpenEDU Model.

If you want to get started right away, ask yourself the following questions:

1. What sets your institution apart from your competition?

Why would someone choose your school over your competitors? Answering this honestly should help you define your brand platform.

2. What kinds of conditions and/or forces do you have to deal with?

Specifically:

- What's your budget?

- When do you need to have your marketing program in place? (In other words, what's your timeline?)

- What are you trying to accomplish? Be as specific as possible. Do you want awareness? Leads? Alumni participation? If you're not sure about your goal, you won't get anywhere.

- What's your brand? How do people feel when they come into contact with your institution/college/school/program? How do you want them to feel?

3. Once you understand what you're up against, what's the big idea that's going to bind your marketing program together?

If you can't explain your strategy in a sentence or two, it's too complicated. You should be able to articulate the reason behind what you're doing — and generally what you're going to do — in the character limit of a tweet.

4. Finally, how are you going to construct the three pillars of your program?

- What kind of traffic do you need to generate? How are you going to generate that traffic?

- What kind of destination are you going to create to receive the traffic that you generate? A landing page? An archived webinar? An open house? Make sure that you are clear about where the people you attract are supposed to go.

- Once you have a destination to capture information from the traffic you generate, how are you going to nurture the leads you generate in order to meet your goal(s)? Email? Social media? Print mailings? Phone calls? In-person visits with candy and flowers? There's no one right way. The trick is to do what works best for your audience(s).

While we know that changing your approach to marketing is a lot more complicated than answering a few questions, those questions are still a major part of the process. If you can define how you're going to generate traffic based on the audiences you're trying to reach, be clear about what kind of destination you're going to send the traffic to, and then know how you're going to nurture those first tentative contacts into enrolled students, you'll be well on your way to successfully applying the OpenEDU Model.

We're not saying it's simple — marketing rarely is, especially higher ed marketing — but it doesn't have to be the giant furball it so often turns into. Define objectives and stay true to them. Understand the constraints you're working under. Develop (and get consensus) on the Big Idea that's going to guide what you need to do.

Nobody may care about your university now, but if you apply what you've learned here, they will.

APPENDIX 1:
BEING A GOOD CLIENT

177

**Over the last 20-plus years, our team has learned —
sometimes the hard way — that relationships
between clients and firms are delicate. They depend
on so much. Chemistry. Honesty. Accountability.
Trust. Respect. Understanding. If one element is
missing, it can sabotage the others, quickly.**

We're extremely lucky when it comes to client relationships. Like, play-the-lottery-now lucky. But when we unpack the strong connections we have with our clients, we find that most of them started strong. They picked us as much as we picked them. A good partner makes a good partnership. For our first lesson in Client 101, let's start with a few recommendations for picking the right agency partner.

The Mythology of the Perfect Partner

Imagine a leprechaun on the back of a unicorn. Now imagine that unicorn riding a dragon. Finding the perfect marketing firm may seem as mythically impossible, but there are a number of steps you can take to end up with a good relationship and not one that leads to endless frustration, costing you time, money, brand equity, and your internal credibility.

Here are six golden rules to help you find that not-so-mythical right fit.

1. Be honest.

If your institutional culture is fast-and-furious, be demanding; if the pace is more gradual, drag your feet. See how a potential partner responds. Can they match your pace? Do they get irritated? Do they seem to understand? If they take issue with how you work before they land your work, they're going to be downright toxic after you hire them.

2. Share the risk.

Everyone knows that there is risk associated with signing a marketing firm, but you might not realize that the firm is also taking a risk signing on with you. What if you want 24/7 service? What if you don't like any of the work and are unable to communicate why? What if you're a monster? What if your funding dries up? Acknowledging that there is risk for both parties and openly talking about it should stimulate an honest discussion that can serve as the framework for mitigating some of that risk together.

3. Ask tough questions.

It's easy to be awesome when things are awesome, but how will the firm behave when the wheels come spinning off? Give them a tough scenario and ask them how they would handle it. Insist on specifics.

4. Ask to meet the team — the REAL team.

Agencies are notorious for sending their A-team of slick sales people and top talent to pitches. Who can blame them? They need to make an airtight case for you to hire them and they're not going to land many accounts with a junior copywriter and a social media coordinator whose college ID hasn't expired yet.

Not surprisingly, many organizations take the bait. They award the work to the A-team. And, far too often, they'll never see those people again.

The school's marketing team is astonished when they sit down to that first kickoff meeting after the contract is signed, only to find the B-team of lower-level staff who can count their years of experience on their fingers and still have plenty of hand left.

5. Try, then buy.

If you have the time and money, hire two or three firms for short, one-off projects. Something small and quick. If you really want to push it, give them the option to pick between two small projects such as one that appeals to emotion or another that requires a more rational, data-driven approach. Note which one they pick, give them a tight deadline, and pay careful attention to what questions they ask and what they ultimately deliver.

Some firms you encounter may choose to exclude themselves from this exercise. That's good for you. If a firm doesn't have the foresight to see the situation as an opportunity to "test drive" the relationship, are they really all that interested in working with you?

6. Don't let yourself be fascinated.

There have been many books written on how to pitch well. Savvy marketing firms practice techniques to make you feel intrigued, dazzled, happy, excited, and hopeful. Their job is to enchant people, whether it's consumers or your marketing team. This is not to say great presenters can't follow through with a great relationship and great work. They can. But fight the urge to give the work to the shiniest firm (it can be tough, we know). Give the work to the most qualified company.

7. Remember: You're hiring a partner, not a vendor.

Make sure you'll be able to work with them. Sure, a great argument can be made that firms that present well will also know how best to sell your products and services. But often, as you peel the proverbial onion, you'll get closer to the truth, and it could involve tears. We submit three truths:

- The bigger the firm, the less likely the folks that pulled on your heartstrings will work on your account.

- Unless the delightful people pitching the heck out of you are going to literally take their show on the road, they aren't going to be the ones selling your products and/or services. Their ads are. Know the difference.

- Most of the techniques and characteristics that generate a strong emotional appeal in person don't transfer all that well to a mass communication medium. Expert presenters use a host of verbal and nonverbal techniques to get you to feel what they want you to feel. Don't let yourself get wrapped up. Weigh both the proposal (rational) and the presentation (emotional) as equal parts of the equation and make the best selection based on all the data, not just the presentation.

Who knows, maybe there are leprechauns-riding-unicorns-riding-dragons out there, but in the absence of concrete evidence, do yourself a favor: Pick the best partner for you based on all the evidence, not just how you feel after the pitch.

Working with an Agency

Once you hire an agency, you have to actually work with them. Most of the time, it takes months upon months to select a partner. And, by that time, you're probably behind on your recruitment cycle and things need to move fast. Hopefully you chose wisely, but even if you didn't, you are most likely stuck with this partner for at least a year. So, the question is: How can you structure the relationship to work successfully?

At the root of every good relationship is respect. Respect is a funny thing because it's not the type of thing you can just ask for or easily give. Respect is earned. And it's earned over time. Nevertheless, there are a few things that you can do every day to be respectful.

For example, you can be respectful with your partner's time by making the most out of meetings. Make sure your team is organized and prepared, insist on an agenda (either from the agency or your team), and understand that chaos on your end will eat up your budget and weaken results.

Marketing is a team sport. There is no reasonable expectation that an agency will ever know the ins and outs of your organization as intimately as you do. An honest agency will know and embrace this.

A good client will also understand that the one or two projects they are working on are just one or two projects of tens — or maybe even hundreds — that the agency will work on each year. Agencies might not know all of your particular ins and outs, but they should have considerable experience running similar projects.

This mutual understanding can serve as a tremendous platform for collaboration and leverage. It can be scary to acknowledge that you don't know something or that you don't have as much experience, but the most successful relationships are the ones where honesty rules. Be OK with not knowing everything, and give both yourself and your agency permission to ask for help.

Along the same lines, if you have data or insights that could help the agency do a better job for you, give it to them. And do so regularly and in a timely fashion. Generating primary data takes time and effort. If you've got some already, help advance your outcomes by sharing it with your agency.

Honesty goes a long way in all relationships, but don't misunderstand being honest with being mean. Try to assume the best and confirm the worst. Few things are as uncomfortable as knowing you unjustly accused someone of incompetence or malice.

That said, feel free to be blunt. No one has time for beating around the bush and, as it happens, agencies have thick skins. If something's not working, be upfront and clear about it. Don't wait for things to go downhill. At the first sign of a problem, nip it.

Also, much like good parenting, fighting in front of the kids is never a good idea. Don't put agencies in the middle of internal disagreements. You'll probably be on the clock through it all and, the more time your agency spends as a counselor, the less time they'll have to do research and creative work.

Along the same lines, don't ask agencies to take sides. They should remain objective and be guided by what makes the most sense for your institution. If you allow them to keep an independent position, they'll have broader credibility when they take on other issues that impact your school.

Finally, define and communicate your expectations for excellence. If you're providing regular feedback and measurements, everyone will stay on the same page. Be clear, reasonable, and fair about the items that your agency should deliver. Ambiguous targets are hard, if not impossible, to hit. Give your agency a fighting chance to be a good partner.

APPENDIX 2:
RESEARCH RESOURCES

185

During the creation of this book, we amassed a catalog of helpful websites. Instead of including the entire list, we've decided to focus on our favorites. Segmented by theme, these compelling sites provide creative inspiration, germane content, and a jolt to spark innovative minds.

Advertising Websites

AdAge (adage.com) is one of the best-known ad industry websites, featuring news, opinion, video of new spots, how-to's, and much more. If it's about advertising and marketing, it's probably here.

AdWeek (adweek.com) has all the latest news from the world of advertising, marketing, and technology, with a large helping of media news tossed in the mix. Much more insider-focused and gossipy than AdAge, AdWeek also offers lots of info about agencies and the people who run them.

SmartBrief (smartbrief.com/industry/marketing-advertising) is a leading digital B2B media company that delivers news and industry insight to over 5 million readers a day.

Business Websites

Bloomberg Business (bloomberg.com) features loads of news from the world of business as well as longer feature articles on hot topics.

Harvard Business Review (HBR) (hbr.org) is the best choice for smart insights and in-depth exploration of hot topics in business and marketing. You'll also find plenty of educational materials if you need to get up to speed on the latest business trends.

Inc.com, from the publisher of *Inc.* magazine, is a great resource for those with an entrepreneurial bent. Anyone running their own business or managing others will find something to inform their day-to-day work-life.

Culture Websites

Cool Hunting (coolhunting.com) is an award-winning publication that has featured the latest in design, technology, style, travel, art, and culture since 2003.

Flavorwire (flavorwire.com) covers media, culture, technology, and creative people from all over the world.

The Verge (theverge.com) focuses on "the intersection of technology, science, art, and culture" with in-depth reporting, feature stories, product information/reviews, and community content.

Education Websites

American Council of Education News (acenet.edu/News-Room/Pages/Todays-Top-Higher-Education-News.aspx) provides a weekly digest of the biggest stories in higher ed curated by the experts at ACE.

The Atlantic Education (theatlantic.com/education) is a subdivision of *The Atlantic* news and opinion publication and provides insights on higher education from top thinkers.

The Chronicle of Higher Education (chronicle.com) is *the* primary higher education industry magazine. While some of the content is free, most of it is subscription-based. *The Chronicle* is also available in print to subscribers.

Educational Technology and Mobile Learning (educatorstechnology.com) is operated by a team of dedicated teachers located in Canada. It serves as a resource of education web tools and mobile apps for teachers and educators.

Inside Higher Ed (insidehighered.com) provides an alternative to *The Chronicle* and does a good job of providing news, insights, and information about trends in higher education while being a bit more irreverent and tech-savvy.

University Business (universitybusiness.com) is a fantastic resource for higher education news, technology, financial issues, policy, and opinion about the business of higher education.

Other Websites

ClickZ (clickz.com) is a treasure trove of advertising/marketing news and insights delivered from some of the top practitioners in the world.

Contently (contently.com/strategist) is a technology company that helps brands create great content at scale. They provide companies technology, content marketing expertise, and creative.

The Daily Dot (dailydot.com) is the ultimate destination for the latest news, opinions, and in-depth reporting from around the internet. No wonder it's known as the hometown newspaper of the World Wide Web.

National Center for Education Statistics (nces.ed.gov) is a data-geek's dream, warehousing all the stats collected by the U.S. government about education. The site also does a good job of analyzing major trends and providing downloadable files containing the data they used to develop their insights.

Reading List

We always note that we built the OpenEDU Model using spare parts from researchers and strategists who came before us. It only makes sense to honor and credit the most influential of the lot by sharing our reading list. As with everything in life, there are things about each book that we will fight to the end for and things we reject outright. It's all part of the process of learning, and we encourage you to take the same approach to the books listed here. Enjoy!

Brainfluence: 100 Ways to Persuade and Convince Consumers with Neuromarketing, Roger Dooley, John Wiley & Sons, 2011.

A good book on neuromarketing that's very tactical. For example, did you know a red button drives more action? Over 20% more action. And that's just one of 99 other neuromarketing-based tips you can find in this book.

Buyology: Truth and Lies About Why We Buy, Martin Lindstrom, Currency, 2008.

This is a fast read about how and why we make "buy" decisions. The insights germinate from an impressive, three-year global neuromarketing study. If you can get past the author's runaway ego and focus squarely on the content, you'll get a lot out of this book.

Contagious: Why Things Catch On, Jonah Berger, Simon & Schuster, 2013.

Berger offers up six rules that govern how content becomes viral. The principles are rooted in memory, psychology, economics, and sociology.

Since many books on our list reference some of the same studies, what you read here may start to sound familiar. We like this book because it structures already familiar concepts and studies to help us craft messages that are not only sticky and effective, but also viral.

David and Goliath: Underdogs, Misfits, and the Art of Battling Giants, Malcolm Gladwell, Little, Brown and Company, 2011.

Gladwell begins his book by retelling a well-known story through a different — and captivating — lens. As it turns out, it wasn't a miracle that David beat Goliath. It just seems like it would have been because he was small and Goliath was big. But David brought a "gun" to a knife fight. Back then, David and other experienced slingers could launch a rock with the stopping power of a .45mm handgun from up to 200 yards away. Goliath didn't have a chance. This book is about how the little guys, more often than not, have the advantage.

Demographics and the Demand for Higher Education, Nathan D. Grawe, Johns Hopkins Press, 2018.

This gem paints a wintery future for higher education. Trending demographic shifts are staging a gigantic pinch on the viability of schools in the Northeast and Midwest. The book also explores how the Great Recession impacted birth rates to further that pinch. The book suggests that schools double down on what makes them unique as the days of "something for everyone" are soon coming to an end.

Drive: The Surprising Truth About What Motivates Us, Daniel H. Pink, Riverhead Books, 2008.

Have you ever wondered how to motivate creative types? It's not always money. Did you know timesheets were an artifact of the industrial revolution? And yet we still use them to measure productivity. Meanwhile, we are thinking about our work in the car, at dinner, in the shower, and elsewhere. What's more, most creative breakthroughs don't happen while on the clock. So, how do you motivate creative people? This book has a lot to say about that.

Fascinate: Your 7 Triggers to Persuasion and Captivation, Sally Hogshead, Harper Business, 2010.

This book is chock-full of very powerful stuff that, when applied properly, can be used for persuasion. The seven triggers are: Innovation, Passion, Power, Prestige, Trust, Mystique, and Alert. Each trigger has its own strategic scaffolding, and we can see entire books written on every one. We like this book because it offers a tactical model for brand positioning and even campaign strategy.

The Laws of Simplicity (Simplicity: Design, Technology, Business, Life), John Maeda, MIT Press, 2006.

Even though this book should have been about fifty pages shorter (keeping with the spirit of the book's title), it offers a number of models that will help you design with simplicity. The author outlines the three laws of simplicity: reduce, organize, and time. It's a tremendous read and we think you'll get a lot out of it.

Made to Stick: Why Some Ideas Survive and Others Die, Chip Heath and Dan Heath, Random House, 2006.

The authors outline a framework that copywriters, marketers, and advertisers can follow to make their messages stickier. If this book reminds of you Malcolm Gladwell's *Tipping Point*, it's because they are very similar in style and content. The Heath brothers draw from psychosocial studies on memory, emotion, and motivation to help us craft and position messages that stay with people.

Present Shock: When Everything Happens Now, Douglas Rushkoff, Riverhead Books, 2008.

Conversation is a dying art form. When people chat and a question comes up that nobody has the answer to, debate, exploration, and critical thinking does not ensue. Instead, someone whips out a mobile phone and Googles the answer. And just like that, the topic, the inquiry, and the intellectual growth opportunity are dead on the spot. There is a generation in the making that is very good at answering questions, but no one commits any of it to memory. That makes it more difficult to connect the dots and think critically. We like this book because it dives into technology and its impact on culture, knowledge, and memory.

Switch: How to Change Things When Change Is Hard, Chip Heath and Dan Heath, Random House, 2010.

This book uses a simple metaphor to help us understand how to get people to switch or change their behavior. Imagine a person riding and guiding an elephant along a path. The Rider represents reason, the Elephant represents emotion, and the Path represents the context in which the desired outcome exists. The basic premise of the book is that change is hard. No one wants to do it, but if you can skillfully direct the Rider, motivate the Elephant, and shape the Path, you might actually be in a position to effect change.

Think Like a Freak: The Authors of Freakonomics Offer to Retrain Your Brain, Steven D. Levitt and Stephen J. Dubner, William Morrow Paperbacks, 2014.

This book encourages you to think against the grain. To think like a child. To ask, "Why?" And to avoid conventional wisdom. We like this book because it gives us techniques for critical thinking and "break[ing] the guessing machine" (see *Made to Stick*). Coincidentally, this can be a good primer for people interested in the foundations of "Design Thinking."

The 22 Immutable Laws of Branding, Al Ries and Laura Ries, Harper Business, 1998.

There are few books about branding that are this pointed and useful. Al and Laura Ries methodically outline the 22 laws of branding. We imagine that the chances of there being exactly 22 laws are very slim. If we had to guess, they chose the number 22 to key off their first book, *The 22 Immutable Laws of Marketing* — which ironically, contradicts immutable branding law *14: The Law of Sub-brands.* They argue, "What branding builds, sub-branding can destroy." Just the same, it's a great book and don't let our persnicketiness rob you from solid fundamentals.

Notes

1. Busta, Hallie. "Tracker: College and University Closings and Consolidation." Education Dive, https://www.educationdive.com/news/tracker-college-and-university-closings-and-consolidation/539961/.

2. This work is provided under the Creative Commons Attribution-ShareAlike 4.0 International licensing terms. Details can be found at https://creativecommons.org/licenses/by-sa/4.0/.

3. Levitt, Steven D.; Dubner, Stephen J. *Freakonomics: A Rogue Economist Explores the Hidden Side of Everything.* HarperCollins, 2009, pg. 87.

4. Taylor, Bill. "How Domino's Pizza Reinvented Itself." Harvard Business Review, 28 Nov. 2016, https://hbr.org/2016/11/how-dominos-pizza-reinvented-itself.

5. Fothergill, David. "Marketing Analysis: Unlocking The Power Of Descriptive Statistics." Marketing Land, 20 Nov. 2015, https://marketingland.com/marketing-analysis-unlocking-power-descriptive-statistics-153045.

6. Discovering Statistics, https://www.discoveringstatistics.com/

7. Huff, Darrell. *How to Lie with Statistics.* Internet Archive, https://archive.org/details/HowToLieWithStatistics.

8. Timoner, Ondi, director. *We Live in Public.* https://www.documentarystorm.com/We-Live-in-Public/, 30 Aug. 2009.

9. Kazmucha, Allyson. "Best IPad Apps for Cats: Pocket Pond 2, Magic Piano, Paint for Cats, and More!" IMore, Dec. 4, 2013, http://www.imore.com/best-ipad-apps-cats-pocket-pond-2-magic-piano-paint-cats-and-more.

10. "Nielsen-Traditional-TV-Viewing-in-Q3-2018-Apr2019." Marketing Charts, 30 Mar. 2019, https://www.marketingcharts.com/charts/us-adults-traditional-tv-viewing-figures-trends-age-q3-2018/attachment/nielsen-traditional-tv-viewing-in-q3-2018-apr2019.

11. "EMarketer-Daily-Media-Time-Estimates-Jun2019." Marketing Charts, 7 June 2019, https://www.marketingcharts.com/charts/us-adults-daily-media-time-estimates-in-2019/attachment/emarketer-daily-media-time-estimates-jun2019.

12. "Research Peek of the Week: Simultaneous Use of Digital Devices While Watching TV Is Common Among U.S. Adults." IIA, 13 Feb. 2019, https://internetinnovation.org/general/research-peek-of-the-week-simultaneous-use-of-digital-devices-while-watching-tv-is-common-among-u-s-adults/

13. "Demographics of Mobile Device Ownership and Adoption in the United States." Pew Research Center: Internet, Science & Tech, 12 June 2019, https://www.pewinternet.org/fact-sheet/mobile/.

14. "Outlook Segment Findings." PwC, https://www.pwc.com/gx/en/industries/tmt/media/outlook/segment-findings.html.

15. Bangah, CJ, et al. "Getting Personal Putting the Me in Entertainment and Media." PwC, https://www.pwc.com/gx/en/entertainment-media/outlook-2019/entertainment-and-media-outlook-perspectives-2019-2023.pdf.

16. "Consumer Intelligence Series: Prepare for the Voice Revolution." PwC, https://www.pwc.com/us/en/services/consulting/library/consumer-intelligence-series/voice-assistants.html.

17. Westlake, Adam. "Amazon Confirms Alexa Device Sales Numbers, and It's a Lot." SlashGear, SlashGear, 5 Jan. 2019, https://www.slashgear.com/amazon-confirms-alexa-device-sales-numbers-and-its-a-lot-05560097/.

18. Smith, Aaron. "U.S. Smartphone Use in 2015." Pew Research Center: Internet, Science & Tech, 3 Jan. 2018, http://www.pewinternet. org/2015/04/01/us-smartphone-use-in-2015/.

19. "SEO vs. PPC – Which Provides You the Better Value?" New Media Campaigns, https://www.newmediacampaigns.com/page/seo-vs-ppc---which-provides-you-the-better-value.

20. Lieberman, Mike. "10 Stats About Inbound Marketing That Will Make Your Jaw Drop." Hubspot, 20 Jan. 2014, https://blog.hubspot.com/insiders/inbound-marketing-stats.

21. Braziel, Lisa. "Social Ad Spending Report – What You Need to Know." Ignite Social Media Agency, 11 Feb. 2019, https://www.ignitesocialmedia.com/social-advertising/social-ad-spending-trends-2019/.

22. Moorman, Christine. "The CMO Survey Highlights and Insights Report - Feb 2019." LinkedIn SlideShare, 3 May 2019, https://www.slideshare.net/christinemoorman/the-cmo-survey-highlights-and-insights-report-feb-2019-143475387?qid=2420383b-3c45-4025-83d3-da18b9398aca&v=&b=&from_search=1.

23. Hosie, Rachel. "An Instagram Star with 2 Million Followers Couldn't Sell 36 T-Shirts, and a Marketing Expert Says Her Case Isn't Rare." Business Insider, Business Insider, 30 May 2019, https://www.businessinsider.com/instagrammer-arii-2-million-followers-cannot-sell-36-t-shirts-2019-5.

24. Stelzner, Michael. "2019 Social Media Marketing Industry Report." Social Media Marketing | Social Media Examiner, 31 May 2019, https://www.socialmediaexaminer.com/social-media-marketing-industry-report-2019/.

25. Bulmer, Don. "The Social Consumer Study." LinkedIn SlideShare, 14 Sept. 2014, http://www.slideshare.net/dbulmer/the-social-consumer-study-091414-2.

26. "The Power of Brand Purpose." Accenture, 5 Dec. 2018, https://www.accenture.com/us-en/insights/strategy/brand-purpose?c=us_us_globalconsumerp_10442470&n=psgs_generic_1218&gclid=CjwKCAjwg-DpBRBbEiwAEV1_-JYwM2h91X0KKCRcjoz7sjxKenovTrNJ2fnntpVYyrq2waHRWuyKEBoCV0gQAvD_BwE.

27. "Are Store Associates Equipped to Deliver Memorable Customer Experiences?" Loyalty360, http://loyalty360.org/resources/article/are-store-associates-equipped-to-deliver-memorable-customer-experiences.

28. Terlep, Sharon. "Everyone Hates Customer Service. This Is Why." The Wall Street Journal, Dow Jones & Company, 3 Aug. 2019, https://www.wsj.com/articles/everyone-hates-customer-service-this-is-why-11564804882.

29. Ruffalo Noel Levitz & OmniUpdate. (2019). 2019 E-expectations trend report. Cedar Rapids, Iowa: Ruffalo Noel Levitz. Available at www.RuffaloNL.com/Expectations

30. Williams, Robert. "Study: Gen Z Prefers Social Media as Top Influence Channel." Marketing Dive, 25 July 2019, https://www.marketingdive.com/news/study-gen-z-prefers-social-media-as-top-influence-channel/559487/.

31. "Gen Z Purchases Largely Influenced by Social Media: National Merchants." National Merchants Association, 11 Aug. 2017, https://www.nationalmerchants.com/gen-z-purchases-largely-influenced-social-media/.

32. "Credibility of a Peer Endorser and Advertising Effectiveness." Journal of Consumer Marketing, https://www.emerald.com/insight/content/doi/10.1108/JCM-11-2014-1221/full/html?mobileUi=0&journalCode=jcm.

33. Hosie, Rachel. "Why Brands Are Turning Away from Big Instagram Influencers to Work with People Who Have Small Followings Instead," Business Insider, 9 Apr. 2019, https://www.businessinsider.com/brands-turning-to-micro-influencers-instead-of-instagram-stars-2019-4?r=US&IR=T.

34. "The Story Behind 'The Furrow', the World's Oldest Content Marketing." Contently, 1 Feb. 2017, http://contently.com/strategist/2013/10/03/the-story-behind-the-furrow-2/.

35. Sheridan, Marcus. "The Story of Marcus Sheridan Carrying the Message of Inbound Marketing to the World." YouTube, 9 June 2016, https://www.youtube.com/watch?v=bINmMQ5_XTc.

36. Burrell, Darcie. "Margot Vs Lily Episode 1: Resolutions." YouTube, 22 Apr. 2016, https://www.youtube.com/watch?v=9XB-qtSaYW0.

37. Danziger, Pamela N. "Nike Outranks Adidas, Under Armour And Lululemon Where It Counts Most: Consumer Perception." Forbes, Forbes Magazine, 23 May 2019, https://www.forbes.com/sites/pamdanziger/2019/05/23/nike-outranks-adidas-under-armour-and-lululemon-where-it-counts-most-consumer-perception/#fbe8df32478a.

38. Ali, Fareeha. "Target's Web Sales Grow More than 25% for Five Years in a Row." Digital Commerce 360, 5 Mar. 2019, https://www.digitalcommerce360.com/2019/03/05/targets-web-sales-grows-more-than-25-for-five-years-in-a-row/.

39. "2019 Nonprofit Benchmarks." M R Benchmarks Study 2019, https://mrbenchmarks.com/words/ways-of-looking.

40. Volovich, Kristina. "What's a Good Clickthrough Rate? New Benchmark Data for Google AdWords." HubSpot Blog, https://blog.hubspot.com/agency/google-adwords-benchmark-data.

41. "What Is a Good Average Landing Page Conversion Rate in 2019?" IMPACT, https://www.impactbnd.com/blog/what-is-a-good-landing-page-conversion-rate.

42. "Screen Resolution Stats Worldwide." StatCounter Global Stats, https://gs.statcounter.com/screen-resolution-stats.

43. Desjardins, Jeff. "How Much Data Is Generated Each Day?" World Economic Forum, https://www.weforum.org/agenda/2019/04/how-much-data-is-generated-each-day-cf4bddf29f/.

44. Devereux-Mack, Hugh. "The Library of Alexandria and Disaster Recovery." Maxava, 19 Sept. 2016, https://maxava.com/2015/09/01/library-alexandria-disaster-recovery/.

45. Crevier, Daniel. *AI: The Tumultuous Search for Artificial Intelligence.* BasicBooks, 1993, pg, 109.

idfive

idfive is an integrated marketing and social design agency for brands on a mission. Born in the Digital Age and raised in Baltimore, Maryland, the agency serves education, health, and nonprofit brands across the United States. idfive blends research, user experience, and emotion-driven creative to connect people to messages and actions that make a difference. The agency's team of researchers, educators, strategists, and creatives are each driven to make a positive dent in the world through projects that include web design and development, cross-channel communications, audience engagement, media planning, and brand strategy. idfive has been recognized for its award-winning work, company culture, and commitment to brands they believe in.